SPEAK UP

A Young Adult's Guide to
**Engage in Difficult Conversation,
Address Conflict, and Earn Respect**

JARED PETERS

ISBN: 978-1-7376188-0-5, 979-8473546224 (paperback)

DEDICATION

For my best friend, Chase. This book would not exist without you.

FREE SCENARIO GUIDE

Want to test your communication skills?

The **Scenario Guide** outlines Jared's **Speak Up Framework** and 13 scenarios to help you conquer the difficult conversations in your life.

You can download the FREE Speak Up Scenario Guide at

https://mailchi.mp/bd84f78cb93b/speak-up-scenario-guide
or at https://jaredpeters.co/free-guide/

CONTENTS

Step 4
Prepare Your Words

Step 5
Speak Up

CHAPTER 1

Introduction

Imagine striding towards your boss's office. You cross through the rows of cubicles with the focus of an archer directed at a target. On the outside, you are calm and collected, but on the inside, you feel your heart thumping. After too many nights at the office until midnight, you know that today is the day you need to ask for a reduction in hours. You knock on the glass sliding door in front of your boss's office and slowly pull it open after you hear, "Come in!"

Ten minutes later, you strut out of the office with your head held high because you get to leave at 4 p.m. every day for the next week, and your boss promised to add another employee to the team in the next month or two to help with the heavy workload. You just nailed the conversation!

Unfortunately, too many young adults shy away from difficult conversations like this one.

What constitutes a difficult conversation?

1. There is possible tension.
2. You feel the need to speak up but don't want to.

A difficult conversation holds possible tension between you and the other person. There are most likely differing opinions and viewpoints that could lead to friction and conflict. This tension is possible because you may not know if the person agrees with you until you enter the conversation. Also, deep down you feel the need to say something even though you don't want to make yourself vulnerable. You don't want to speak up, but you know that you need to.

A difficult conversation could be a conversation with your boss about burnout or a raise. It could be asking your coach for more playing time on the court or a different position in the field. Maybe your professor gave you a terrible grade on a paper and you want to plead your case for a higher score. Possibly, you have that one roommate who always leaves his or her dirty dishes in the sink and it is time to put your foot down.

When faced with a difficult conversation with your boss, coach, or friend, do you bite your tongue instead of sharing what needs to be said? Rather than bringing up your honest feedback and opinion, you hold in your feelings. Maybe the issue you want to address blows over, but more than likely you hold on to some type of bitterness and put up with the same problem over and over again.

You may feel quiet, unassertive, or terrible at addressing conflict. You hold back out of fear of hurting a relationship, hurting someone's feelings, or not wanting to say the wrong thing. Maybe you are afraid of punishment from the other person if you truly share what is on your mind.

That used to be me. I avoided conflict at all costs and be-came a doormat for others to walk all over. I'll never forget the day when I sat in the student center on campus with my ex-girlfriend and some of her friends. As I met these friends for the first time, she proceeded to tell them about me. One statement she mentioned still sticks with me today, "Jared is a pushover. That's one of the things I like most about him. Just kidding." While she said it as a joke and meant no harm, that comment hurt because I knew it was true.

I gritted my teeth in an awkward smile and half-heartedly enjoyed a fake laugh with everyone else, but deep down I wanted to leave. Guess what? I never told her that comment bothered me. Throughout the six months that we dated, I never shared that I didn't like being called a pushover and it made me feel like I was being taken advantage of.

This book is for young adults who want to conquer silence and earn respect—the students, athletes, and young pro-fessionals who want to stand up for themselves. Those of you who run scenario after scenario in your mind about what you need to say but never follow through. Even after approaching a difficult conversation, you leave disappointed because you did not say what needed to be said. This is not for the professional who has been working for 20 years. Difficult conversations reach another level at that stage of life and present their own set of challenges.

Speak Up outlines the tools and framework you need to navigate the difficult conversations in your young adult life. It shows you why you are shying away and acknowledges the costs of doing so. This book outlines five clear steps to approach and word a conversation to help you earn respect.

This will not be a book just giving you encouragement to speak up. It outlines a framework you can apply during the moments when you are not sure what to say. Instead of walking away from a conversation feeling disappointed for not speaking up, you will leave with the confidence and respect you deserve.

Once that dating relationship ended, I knew that something needed to change. My best friend and college roommate, Chase, is great at addressing conflict head on. I told him that I need to be better at facing conflict, and he helped shape me over the next three years. Chase helped put me in situations where I was uncomfortable and forced me to engage in tough conversations. As I gained more practice with conflict, I found that I was already extremely effective at navigating difficult conversations. I knew how to think from the other person's point of view, consider a message, and deliver in a specific way depending on the situation and person in front of me. I just needed a friend to hold me accountable and push me to stand up for myself.

At first, I was just doing what I thought would be right in the midst of conflict or difficult conversations. When I started diving into the process and researching the best approaches for handling tough conversations, I found that top conflict resolution and management consulting companies recommend the steps outlined in this book.

I competed as a NCAA Division I athlete in college. Through years of athletics, I saw the benefits of healthy conflict on teams. While most years of college athletics were great for my team, we went through a coaching change ahead of my senior season. I witnessed more conflict in that one year than most teams experience in four. Issues were caused by both the coaches and the athletes, and I had a front-row seat for some of the greatest observation into conflict and difficult conversations.

After graduating college, I completed an intense training program at one of the largest banks in the United States. Through the program, I reported to upwards of 10 different managers or rotation-leads in a single year and honed the ability to communicate with different leaders in different ways.

People always ask me for help with wording a message. Everything from an email to another coworker to the text message to the guy or girl that my friend wants to take on a date. Chase and I ran a clinic in college where our friends sat on our dorm room double-decker couch and we helped them word the text messages and conversations in their lives.

During the first year of my professional career, I sat down with a manager of mine and held a conversation about feeling burnt out due to late nights in the office. For months afterward, I was told that people my age don't know how to handle conflict with that level of maturity and maybe one other person my age would be able to hold a conversation with as much effectiveness. Plus, the conversation resulted in a necessary decrease in hours.

The same framework that helped me decrease my hours has worked for young professionals, athletes, and conversations with friends. The tools in this book helped coworkers succeed in stressful conversations with clients and teammates. It helped an athletic team be heard and respected on issues that had persisted for months and years. Sarah utilizes a tool in this book that helps her in conversations and even helped her save someone's life. I've shared these tips with my coworkers, friends, and teammates, but now they are in your hands.

I promise that if you follow this framework, you will know exactly what you need to say in a difficult conversation and will walk away feeling relieved that you finally spoke up. You will gain respect from your coaches, teammates, and bosses by approaching conflict with a mature perspective that isn't seen in most young adults. This book doesn't just have the ability to change how others perceive you, but how you view yourself.

Don't be the person who keeps sitting on his hands in the back of the room without sharing what is on his mind. Don't be the one who goes weeks or months wishing she had said something to her boss but keeps putting up with the same issues for far too long. Don't be the person who enters a conversation and handles it so poorly that nothing changes and everything operates as if nothing happened.

Be the young adult who stands out. Be the one who stands up for yourself. Be the only person in your work team who is willing to push back and make ideas and processes better. Be the one who others go to for advice because your friends and teammates can't help but notice how effectively you communicate with those around you.

Utilize the framework and the communication tools you are about to read that have been proven to improve effectiveness in tough conversations. All you need to do to learn the framework and mindset to approach a difficult conversation in your life is to keep reading. Each chapter contains keys to remember, questions to ask yourself, and a practice scenario for you to think through to help you take action towards what you have put off for far too long.

SPEAK UP FRAMEWORK

Step 1: **Understand**
Understand the importance of speaking up and
why people avoid difficult conversations.

Step 2: **Prepare Your Heart**
Prepare yourself for the conversation.

Step 3: **Prepare the Environment**
Set the correct stage for the conversation.

Step 4: **Prepare Your Words**
Discover the words for your conversation.

Step 5: **Speak Up**
Take action.

Step 1
UNDERSTAND

— — —

Understand the importance of speaking up and
why people avoid difficult conversations.

CHAPTER 2

Why Speak Up?

For my first job in college, I worked as a sales associate at the local running store in my hometown. Before I was let loose to sell running shoes to customers, I studied the intricacies of shoe models for a week through an online learning portal.

On my first day, I strolled to the back room, plopped down on the 30-year-old swivel chair, and clicked the spacebar to open the computer. Instead of starting on the online portals, I realized there was a password standing between me and the Internet. Rather than standing up and finding my boss for the password, I sat and made a few guesses before I waited for 5–10 minutes for him to magically appear.

Eventually, my boss passed through my part of the store and asked how I was doing. I mentioned that I needed the password to get into the computer, and he told me some-thing I will never forget, "I won't know that I need to help you unless you say something."

I wasn't great at communicating with him the rest of the summer, but I still think about that quote to this day. When I don't know whether I should say something or if someone else understands me, I ask myself, "Do I need to say some-thing for the other person to know what I'm thinking?"

Speaking up is vital to the success of any team. In order for a team to function successfully, you have to share what is on your mind. You must share what you need to be success-ful. People don't know that you need help unless you say something.

As much as some people in dating relationships or marriages expect their significant other to know what they are think-ing or feeling at all times, people don't know what you are thinking. You will not know exactly what the other person is thinking unless they say it. I am a twin, and even through twin telepathy, my brother and I can't tell what the other is thinking 100% of the time.

Your boss is not sitting around thinking about your feelings all day. Your coach is not spending his or her free time think-ing about if you have exactly what you need to be prepared for the workout the next day. Your teacher doesn't sit in her office thinking about whether you understand the fifth sen-tence on a PowerPoint in the middle of a lecture. Your coach, manager, or leader is not a mind reader. The quickest way for your needs and wants to be heard is to speak up.

While sitting at a computer for 5–10 minutes trying to guess a password is not costing the company a lot of money on a minimum-wage paycheck, not speaking up at other moments may. Imagine being tasked with a project where you have to present to an executive in your company but your boss does not share the correct shared drive with the information you need. Imagine you were told to update a pitchbook for a client meeting and your boss did not give you the previous version that she told you to build on.

Every day you will be faced with moments where it is helpful to speak up quickly and effectively. The better you are at sharing what you need or what you think, the more time, money, and stress you can save yourself and your team.

The Cost of Avoiding

In a 2018 study, researchers examined the effects of a delay in speaking up. They call the gap between the time a problem is identified and the time the problem is discussed as the *Accountability Gap.* Healthier companies have a shorter accountability gap and discuss issues in a timely and effective manner. Unhealthy companies have a longer accountability gap where it takes longer to bring issues to the table.

"In the study of 792 professionals, 52 percent of employees hesitate to discuss peer performance problems, 55 percent are reluctant to discuss when they believe someone makes a bad strategic choice, and 49 percent take more than a week to speak up when policy decisions are beginning to create unintended negative consequences."[1]

The delay in sharing concerns translates into inefficiencies for your company. It is costing you and your team thousands of dollars every time it takes multiple days to speak up about issues or unintended consequences.

"When three days or fewer pass between the identification of a problem and a frank, honest and respectful conversation about it, roughly $5,000 is wasted, according to the survey data. However, when the accountability gap reaches five days or more, employees estimate more than $25,000 is wasted."[1]

People sit around and let little moments of frustration or miscommunication boil over into massive inefficiencies. Every time you delay sharing needed, constructive feedback for a problem with a project, you cost your company precious time, energy, and stress. You will have times in the workplace where you do not agree with how a team is handling new processes. You will notice little behaviors and actions of coworkers that cause errors. The more consistent you become with sharing necessary feedback and ideas, the more time and stress you will save yourself.

---

[1] Maxfield, D., & Willis, S. (2018, July 11). *Long silences at work: Companies struggle when employees don't quickly surface problems or concerns.* VitalSmarts. https://www.vitalsmarts.com/press/2018/07/long-silences-at-work/

You may be afraid of conflict, but it is a necessary part of any successful team. Jon Gordon is a best-selling author, speaker, and consultant for teams across the country. He works with Fortune 500 companies and professional sports teams like the Los Angeles Dodgers, Miami Heat, and Clemson Football. When asked about a common element of successful teams, he first mentioned the ability to have healthy conflict.

A tough conversation may hurt you and the other person a little bit, but the costs related to holding your tongue for years will hurt even more. We can say, "I'll deal with it later," but we often never do. The stress of putting off conflict builds on your body. It breaks you down and eats away at your mind and heart.

I experienced moments where I lied in bed for hours without sleeping because I could not stop thinking about how I avoided saying what I wanted. I replayed conversations over and over in my head because I knew I did not get my point across and avoided saying what needed to be said. I felt like I was misunderstood and disrespected because I could never stand up for myself. I have felt that pit in my stomach and the shaking of my knees from pure fear of speaking up. The longer you put off necessary conversations, the more stress you put on yourself.

That pit in your stomach is the reason you should speak up. It may not be a multi-million-dollar deal or the largest product rollout in your company's history, but you will be there someday. You will be the one who needs to combine teams together to meet a big deadline or close a large deal.

You will be the one to hire and fire employees. Learning how to communicate what you need is important because you do not have to sit awake at night mulling over the conversation you had earlier in the day. You do not need to leave a conversation feeling like you never got your point across.

One conversation can save you hours of frustration. When I started college, I was thrown into a dorm with another person for the first time since my twin brother and I split rooms. The first couple weeks of school, my roommate would leave for an 8 a.m. class (a rookie scheduling mistake), but on his way out, the door would slam and wake me up.

It didn't help that we lived in the most run-down dorm on campus, so the doors and frames were not exactly the highest quality. The handle would jolt the last bit and make a louder-than-necessary sound if you closed it with normal force. Even though something like closing a door during a normal part of the day would not be an issue, it can get annoying when you are trying to sleep in the morning. After a week of putting up with being woken up in the morning, I simply asked him if he could try to close the door quieter on his way out.

He did not realize that it was loud, and the door noise was not a problem the rest of the year. The conversation may have taken a little courage on my part, but a 20-second conversation saved months of frustration.

There are going to be numerous versions of annoying doors that pop up in life, and a quick conversation can save you hours, weeks, or months of frustration.

Desired Skill

Guess what is always one of the most desired skills by recruiters for new hires? Communication.[2] Why? Communication is the basis of every team. You need to be able to communicate your thoughts in a way that others understand and to convince others that your work is worth trusting. You need to be able to email, call, or talk to people to get the information needed to complete a task or help someone finish a project.[3]

I recently finished a year-long training program at one of the largest banks in the country. In the program, I had a difficult conversation about how I was feeling. I communicated that I needed a temporary change to bring the most effectiveness to the team. The conversation resulted in some changes for me and the team that helped us work better for the rest of my rotation. Afterward, I was told, "Those conversations don't happen. Few people have the maturity as a young analyst to share something in such an effective way." That one conversation elevated my confidence in my job and improved my performance for the last five months of my training rotations.

---

[2] Indeed Editorial Team. (2020, December 1). *Top 11 skills employers look for in candidates.* Indeed Career Guide. https://www.indeed.com/career-advice/resumes-cover-letters/skills-employers-look-for

[3] Doyle, A. (2021, June 2). *Do you have the top skills employers want?* The Balance Careers. https://www.thebalancecareers.com/top-skills-employers-want-2062481

People will notice when you can speak up effectively. They will notice when you can communicate what you need while also looking out for those around you.

Your boss is not looking for a bunch of yes men or women. Your boss wants people who will push back on ideas to make them better. You can sit back and nod your head in agreement during every meeting or you can throw out ideas that contribute to your team. You will not have the perfect answer most of the time, but you can start conversations that lead to even better ideas.

From 2002–2016, Wells Fargo incentivized sales employees through the number of new accounts opened. Bank employees earn large compensation through bonuses; therefore, the greater the number of new accounts opened, the larger the check in the sales officers' pockets at the end of the year. Unfortunately, the company set unrealistic sales goals that led to fraudulent activity by company employees. Accounts were opened by employees for unknowing account holders like you and me. To meet goals, they opened millions of accounts without consent through forged signatures and other forms of fake identification. At the beginning of 2020, Wells Fargo agreed to $3 billion in settlement charges related to the fraudulent account over those 14–15 years.[4]

---

[4]   Flitter, E. (2020, February 22). *The price of Wells Fargo's fake account scandal grows by $3 billion.* The New York Times. https://www.nytimes.com/2020/02/21/business/wells-fargo-settlement.html

In 2018, a Boeing flight surprisingly crashed near Indonesia. In 2019, another commercial Boeing flight crashed shortly after takeoff. Both crashes killed every passenger on board and both flights were Boeing 737 MAX planes. After investigations, it was discovered that the crashes were linked to the operation of something called the Maneuvering Characteristics Augmentation System (MCAS). The flight system had technical malfunctions that caused the flights to crash in rare situations. Boeing employees failed to disclose concerns about MACS, and Boeing agreed to pay $2.5 billion in settlements. During further investigation, Boeing also grounded all 737 MAX flights while experts fixed the planes' software errors.[5]

Not only did these mistakes cost the companies billions of dollars, but even more beyond settlements due to damaged reputation. If more employees spoke up about software concerns in Boeing 737 MAX planes, 346 lives could have been saved and millions of dollars in losses from grounded flights and plane crashes could have been avoided. Wells Fargo reached a $3 billion settlement related to fraudulent account openings. If sales employees at Wells Fargo spoke up about the improper nature of their incentives, the company could have saved billions of dollars in lawsuits and a damaged reputation.

---

[5]   Office of Public Affairs. (2021, January 7). *Boeing charged with 737 MAX fraud conspiracy and agrees to pay over 2.5 billion*. The United States Department of Justice. https://www.justice.gov/opa/pr/boeing-charged-737-max-fraud-conspiracy-and-agrees-pay-over-25-billion

I have seen firsthand that young adults joining the workforce often have not been taught how to handle difficult conversations. Few people bring up their true feelings in situations where there is tension or differing opinions, and even fewer do it effectively.

Remember:

- People cannot read your mind. Others do not know to help you unless you say something.
- Remaining silent costs your company $1,000s of dollars every day an issue persists.

Questions to Ask Yourself:

- Do I need to say something for the other person to know what I am thinking?
- Could a problem be solved quicker if I ask for help or clarification?

Scenario:

You work in a sales associate role at a department store, and you are supposed to restock a clothing section but can't find the shirts to put on the racks. You don't remember where your boss told you to look and cannot find the shirts in the storage area. You don't want to waste an hour digging through storage, but you also don't want to ask your boss for instructions a second time. What would you do?

CHAPTER 3

Why We Avoid Difficult Conversations

During my sophomore year of high school, I sat in the top row of the computer lab for my accounting class. On a typical Tuesday, I prepared for class like any other day. I adjusted my creaky, old chair and logged into the ancient box-shaped computer monitor that took forever for the screen to warm up. All of a sudden, the guy who sat two seats down from me, we will call him Josh for this story, burst into the classroom shaking and raging with bloodshot eyes. Instead of going straight to his seat, he planted himself in front of me and stared into my soul like Nicholas Cage in *Ghost Rider*.

Josh hurled insults and threats at me for two minutes straight as I sat clenching the armrests of my seat. I was called names that I will not repeat and was told to never say anything about him ever again or he would seriously injure me. Thankfully, a track teammate of mine sat in between Josh and myself and calmed him down enough to keep him from physically harming me.

I sat for the rest of class with Josh's eyes pierced into the side of my head as I tried to focus on balancing ledgers. From the pelting of verbal insults to feeling as if I were this man's prey, I was never more thrilled to get out of class that day.

This traumatizing encounter transpired because of a conversation I had the day before with Josh's girlfriend. She was really good friends with one of my teammates and best friends, so I would talk to her once in a while after lunch. The day before Josh's threats, I walked out of the lunchroom as some of my friends stood with Josh's girlfriend and motioned for me to join the conversation. As I joined the circle, I was asked to tell her what I knew about this guy she had been dating.

Since I sat close enough to Josh in accounting class, I overheard some of his locker room talk. Some of his extracurricular activities, to say it nicely, were not the greatest choices in the world. Since I cared about her and one of my best friends insisted, I shared some of the things I overheard from a couple chairs down. She refused to believe me and mentioned that Josh told her he did not do any of those things anymore. I ended my sharing there, but clearly she went and had a conversation with Josh later that day.

It was a recipe for disaster from the beginning. That day in class was the closest I have ever felt to being beaten up, and it was the most verbal abuse I have ever taken in my life. The rampage came because I spoke up and shared some things I had heard in class. I can look back on this time and see that it made it harder for me to speak up over the following few years. My mind even forgets about the memory from time to time.

Long-Term Effects

I was scared to share controversial information for a long time. My experience in high school made it difficult to speak up because deep down part of me feared I could experience verbal abuse if I said the wrong thing to the wrong person.

We each have different reasons for why we avoid difficult conversations. Commonly, there may be a time in your childhood where you spoke up and were humiliated or shamed. Your actions may be driven by how your family communicates with one another. If your family is confrontational growing up, you are often more comfortable addressing difficult conversations because you witnessed that on a daily basis. For others, you may have a family full of parents and siblings who shy away from conflict at any cost.

Your family upbringing factors into your ability to address tough conversations. If you come from a family of challengers and arguers, then you may be more comfortable speaking up, but you may also bite your tongue if that was taken to the extreme. You may come from a family that avoids conflict so you do not know what it looks like to consistently hold healthy disagreements. Conflict in those situations can often be seen as scary, unnecessary, or damaging. Some individuals were constantly under a microscope by their parents and don't want to speak up out of a fear of punishment.

I come from a family with a lot of natural conflict avoiders, so I didn't grow up pushing back or consistently sharing my opinions about things I wanted changed. As I grew older, I learned to recognize the impact of my family environment on how I communicate with others. Now I have to be conscious of my natural tendencies in order to truly speak up for myself.

Some of you may come from families where arguing and confrontation are normal occurrences. You grow up arguing about little disagreements, so conflict does not scare you. In order to keep up with your family, you had to be blunt and direct to get your point acknowledged. While you do not see your approach as bad, you may feel like other people don't understand your direct approach to difficult conversations or conflict.

As you approach a difficult conversation, understand your natural tendencies when facing conflict. Look back at moments that deeply shaped you and understand your family's approach in order to move forward with the confidence you need to speak up.

Research

There are different fears that influence individuals to remain silent in times where they know they should speak up.

In his popular TED Talk, Adam Galinsky shares the dynamics behind speaking up for yourself.[6] In his research, he found the difference between speaking up and remaining silent comes down to the perception of power in the relationship. When you have a low perception of power in the relationship, you feel that there are often two options: speak up and get rejected or remain silent and go unnoticed. In difficult situations, people see a small window of opportunity to communicate their needs and desires effectively between two looming negative outcomes.

The lower the perceived power of the individual, the smaller the window of acceptable behavior. As young adults, we often don't have great power in relationships with our coaches or bosses. Instead of remaining silent, your goal is to communicate effectively in tighter windows of acceptable behavior and minimal power.

Galinsky also highlights one of the biggest reasons people avoid difficult conversations—fear of altering the relationship. Numbers of scientific studies, social psychologists, and my own conversations and surveys indicate that most people

---

[6] Galinsky, A. (2016, November 23). *How to speak up for yourself.* TED Talks. https://www.ted.com/talks/adam_galinsky_how_to_speak_up_for_yourself?language=en#t-256388

avoid conflict and tough conversations out of fear of hurting the relationship with the other person.

Friends have a hard time telling their friends the truth because they don't want to hurt the trust and friendship that is built. Coworkers don't want to give constructive feedback to other coworkers because they do not want to harm the established working relationship.

For example:

Billy's roommate never takes out the trash when the garbage is full and instead piles his paper plates like an accordion, waiting for someone else to do the job. Billy naturally doesn't want to bring up the fact that it bothers him that his roommate won't help out around the apartment because he can easily take out the trash himself.

Courtney's coworker always cuts out of the office early and leaves projects with tight deadlines on Courtney's plate that lead to frustrating late nights at her desk. She doesn't want to speak up because she is young, likes the overtime pay, and doesn't necessarily mind working late.

There are little moments where individuals shy away from conflict out of fear of harming the relationship. Amy K Hutchens dives deeper within the individual desire to keep the relationship and indicates that ego is actually the cause of avoiding conflict.[7] At the end of the day, we avoid speak-

---

[7]   Baker, T. (Host). (2020, September 10). Stop avoiding tough conversations with AmyK Hutchens [Audio podcast episode].

ing up because we want others to like us. Naturally, we want our bosses, friends, and peers to like us.

When people like you, you often receive benefits that are not afforded to others. In sports, you may receive more playing time. In school, you may receive better grades on tests or assignments. At work, you have a greater chance of promotion or a bonus. Subconsciously, you contemplate the benefits of someone liking you before you put that relationship in danger.

Specifically at the office, this fear of not being liked plays a large part in everyday interactions. VitalSmarts found that employees do not speak up at work because they do not believe others would join in support, they expect retaliation, or they are afraid that their career could be damaged.[8]

If you go into a meeting and call out your boss by yelling in his or her face about the company performance, then those fears of retaliation are true. You most likely will not gain much support, will have some type of retaliation, and may even be fired on the spot. However, when you handle conversations with control and grace, the fear of retaliation or career damage should not prevent you from approaching a difficult conversation.

In *Resist Average Academy*. Spotify. https://open.spotify.com/episode/2KqrcQrMHUNSK0mekmh0gk?si=9b6be8b133524875

[8]   Maxfield, D., & Willis, S. (2018, July 11). *Long silences at work: Companies struggle when employees don't quickly surface problems or concerns.* VitalSmarts. https://www.vitalsmarts.com/press/2018/07/long-silences-at-work/

The fears in your brain exist to protect you from pain. Judith Glaser, an organizational anthropologist and author of *Conversational Intelligence*, states, "When we are rejected, we experience pain in the same centers in the brain and body as when we are in a car crash."[9] No wonder heartbreak or being distanced by a friend hurts so bad. We go through an emotional car crash when we are rejected. Your brain likes to be comfortable because it is protecting you from pain.

For natural people-pleasers, you shape your conversations to avoid anything that could make someone dislike you. Know this: being liked and speaking up do not have to be mutually exclusive.

Safety

Culture Code by Daniel Coyle highlights the major elements of effective team cultures.[10] From business to athletics, high performing teams carry certain consistent qualities. One of the main characteristics highlighted in the book is psychological safety.

Harvard Business School professor, Dr. Amy Edmondson, describes psychological safety as "a climate in which people

[9] Glaser, J. (2012). Engage in CHANGES. *Leadership Excellence*, *29*(4). https://conversationalintelligence.com/images/pdf/glaser-featured-author.pdf
[10] Coyle, D. (2018). *The culture code: The secrets of highly successful groups*. Penguin Random House.

are comfortable being (and expressing) themselves."[11] With greater psychological safety, employees and team members experience decreased fear of retaliation and rejection. They feel safe enough to share their thoughts and ideas in a psychologically safe environment.

An underlying factor in your willingness to speak up depends on the safety present in your team or relationship. We each have a boss we do not or did not feel comfortable with sharing our true thoughts or ideas for improvement. We each have friends with which we are scared to share the truth. You often shy away from those necessary conversations because you do not feel safe.

Think about your favorite boss. That person probably made you feel comfortable sharing your opinions or being yourself. They made you feel valued and withheld judgement when you made a mistake. They probably made you feel confident in your abilities and kept personal items between you and them. They showed that they were on your side. When your boss makes you feel safe, you are more likely to speak up.

While psychological safety plays a role in your comfortability to have a difficult conversation, a lot of the pressure is on the other person to foster an environment where team members feel comfortable sharing their honest thoughts and opinions. It is an underlying factor that you should be

---

[11]   Herway, J. (2017, December 7). *How to create a culture of psychological safety.* Gallup. https://www.gallup.com/workplace/236198/create-culture-psychological-safety.aspx

aware of that may be influencing your courage to share what is on your mind.

Psychological safety is a mental/emotional driver of conversations, but physical safety is different. If you feel like you may be physically harmed by speaking up, then get someone else involved. If you believe that there could be a serious retaliation against your choice to share your mind or heart, then involve a professional or someone else who will protect you.

If you are in that difficult situation, entrust an adult who has your best interest at heart. Never put yourself in harm's way by having a difficult conversation. Your life and safety are not worth sacrificing for the sake of sharing every little detail about how you are feeling. Find someone who can help remove you from the situation or enact change on your behalf.

It can be difficult to determine who you can trust when you open up. You don't want to keep everything bottled up, but you also don't want to be let down or betrayed by the wrong person. Renee Slansky, a relationship expert, shares that it is best to open up in phases. If there is someone you want to share valuable information with, you need to develop trust over time. She recommends a phased approach where you share parts of important events or feelings with someone and see how the other person responds. You share little pieces at a time and eventually see if that individual is worth trusting with larger vulnerabilities.[12]

---

[12]   Magnetize Your Main, & Slansky, R. (2021, March 4). *When is it safe to open up to someone? (With Renee Slansky).* Spotify.

If you need a person to go to for safety or help in difficult situations, go to someone who has responded well when you opened up about smaller things in the past. Go to a person who has proven themselves as accepting and helpful when you make yourself vulnerable. You don't want to drop a vulnerability bomb on your boss of one week or a friend you just met. Take time to build a relationship where you feel safe and the other person proves they can be trusted with valuable information. If you need someone quickly, go to a trusted friend or mentor.

Fears and Lies

Whether you had an altering experience growing up or not, you probably have fears or lies you believe that influence how you interact with conflict or address difficult conversations.

As I examined my tendencies, I noticed I believed lies that prevented me from approaching confrontation. I found that I had a judgment wound from "Josh" in my accounting class. I discovered a rejection wound that I had not dealt with from a dating relationship.

These large experiences made me believe that if I ever spoke up I would be judged or rejected. I believed the lies of one-off events that didn't reflect the times when I was accepted

https://open.spotify.com/episode/5eXxSz3pZmKYLTca6T-n3eZ?si=KL4FepeLSuSTmFkK8uj14Q&utm_source=-copy-link&dl_branch=1

and respected. The result of a singular event does not mean you will experience the same pain if you try again.

Common lies we tell ourselves:

- If I share my true feelings, I will be rejected.
- If I pushback on my boss's idea, he/she will not respect my work.
- Difficult conversations mean arguing/yelling.
- I cannot be liked by the other person if I speak up.

Everyone has fears buried deep down that hold them back from having a difficult conversation. You need to be aware of the fears and lies in your head to truly find the power to speak up when the time is right. Awareness begins the months- or years-long journey to truly come to terms with deeply-affecting pain.

These fears and lies come from your brain trying to protect you. Fear is a natural product of doing something that could be dangerous. That is why we commonly hear the phrase, "Get comfortable being uncomfortable." You have to work against your brain to make steps in the right direction. Jon Gordon says that you wouldn't choose to have a negative thought.[13]

---

[13] Gordon, J. (2019, August 11). *Your negative thoughts are not coming from you.* Facebook. https://fb.watch/6dV_JWTFQz/

The fears and lies that pop into your head are a psychological mechanism to try and protect you from the dangerous world.

You would not tolerate a best friend telling you to shy away from everything worth fighting for. If your brother told you that you are destined for rejection, you would get angry with him. If your coworker told you to "shut-up and smile through the pain," you would start looking for a new job. Why do you believe the same thoughts that are created in your head? These thoughts and lies hold you back from saying what needs to be said.

Remember:

- Being liked and speaking up do not have to be mutually exclusive.
- The result of a singular event does not mean you will experience the same pain if you try again.
- A framework helps you focus on the task in front of you instead of the reasons to be scared.

Questions to Ask Yourself:

- Did I have something in my past that makes it harder for me to speak up?
- What lies am I believing about what could happen to me if I share?
- Is it safe for me to speak up?

Scenario:

You are frustrated with your job. You feel like you are being taken advantage of, people don't listen, and you are working an insane number of hours just to meet all of the deadlines and fire drills that show up every day. After some reflection, you realize that you haven't shared any of your true feelings with your boss. How do you approach that conversation?

Step 2
PREPARE
YOUR HEART

– – –

Prepare yourself for the conversation.

CHAPTER 4

Empathy

*U*ndercover Boss took television by storm when it debuted back in 2010. For the show, executives of large U.S. companies disguise themselves and pose as entry-level workers in their own companies. Often, the leaders try to discover underlying reasons why the company is not performing to the desired standards. By pretending to be an entry-level employee, leaders gain a clear picture of day-to-day operations. Episodes included executives from Waste Management, 7-Eleven, DIRECTV, NASCAR, and even the Chicago Cubs.

Mitchell Modell, CEO of Modell's Sporting Goods, went undercover to learn why his company spent so much money on expenses compared to the revenue returned.[14] Modell visited

---

[14] Gonzales, A. (Writer), & Lambert, S. (Director). (2012, November 2). Modell's sporting goods (Season 4, Episode 1)

different individual sporting goods store locations as well as a distribution center. While he went undercover, he encountered numerous staffing and distribution problems that drastically impacted company performance. Modell discovered that one of his store associates was living in a homeless shelter because she couldn't afford to pay rent or a mortgage and also support her family. The CEO was so moved by this associate's work ethic in spite of her struggles that he paid for a house so she would never need to sleep at a homeless shelter again.

Mitchell Modell could have made assumptions about the state of the company without experiencing day-to-day operations for himself. Instead, he placed himself in the shoes of his employees and saw what they experienced. Being in the place of others helped him navigate conversations with his other executives and adjust his company for future success.

Just like CEOs benefit from working alongside their employees, we each benefit from putting ourselves in the shoes of others. Before you approach a difficult conversation, take time to picture yourself in the position of the person you are talking to. Take the time to feel what that person feels and view the situation from a different perspective.

Does the Other Person Understand?

During one of my rotations in the training program, I was tasked with putting together a document highlighting

---

[TV series episode]. In S. Lambert (Executive Producer), *Undercover Boss*. Studio Lambert.

different clients and prospects for a meeting with an internal partner at the bank. The deliverable included data points such as estimates of company revenue, ownership, and a company description. Most of the data was easy to find, but it was difficult to find certain company descriptions.

After I sent the first draft of the spreadsheet over to a banker and mentor of mine, he came over to my desk to review. He circled a couple of company descriptions and asked me if I knew what the description meant. After I admitted that I did not understand how the companies make money, he told me, "You have to picture yourself in the reader's shoes. The goal is to make it as simple as possible." A company may be a manufacturer of athletic socks, but the company description on the website may read, "The world's premier fabric synthesizer through integrated weaving patterns and soft materials." That description sounds sophisticated, but at the end of the day, no one understands what it means.

In any conversation, will the other person understand where you are coming from? Put yourself in his or her shoes and imagine someone approaching you.

One of the best questions I use to ask myself if someone will understand a description is by asking "What does this mean?" I may have a bunch of fancy words to say to other people, but what does it mean to them? Words in your head may not make sense to someone else.

Lack of Information

During my senior year of college, my cross country team held a big team meeting during the middle of the season. At this point, most people on our team were frustrated with a variety of practice and coaching details combined with sub-par performance. The captains set up a time with the coaches and the athletes to sit down and sift through different concerns and issues.

As we all sat down in a classroom on campus, the coaches started by saying they thought everything was going great and were shocked to find out that there are all kinds of issues below the surface that need to be addressed. I saw that day that coaches, managers, and bosses do not know everything you are feeling or thinking. Your boss or coach is not a mind reader. What you think is blatantly obvious may surprise them.

During your mental preparation for a conversation, consider the information you possess that is non-existent to the other party. As you think through other perspectives of the story, you will realize different ideas of how to communicate effectively with the other person.

For a person feeling burnout, your boss or manager probably does not know exactly how you feel. When you put yourself in their shoes, there is a good chance you have not told them you feel exhausted in the middle of the week and work late nights to keep up with project demands. Your approach to a conversation with your boss is different if you consistently asked for time off than if you remained silent about your exhaustion for the last three months.

Perhaps a friend ditched you for another friend after the two of you decided to get dinner later this week. You told them you did not mind them canceling, but deep down you are upset your friend ignored a commitment. If you approach a conversation with that friend, he or she may not know how you felt about ditching you for someone else because you said you didn't mind the cancellation.

When you place yourself in the other person's position, you see how a situation could be perceived from multiple angles. You see your boss's point of view and understand how your friend would react. Feeling empathy opens you to an understanding of how that person would like to be communicated with. It teaches you to remain calm, composed, and respectful.

If you were someone else, you would not want someone accusing you of making mistakes. You would want someone who listens, attempts to understand your point of view, and who respects you as an individual. You would want someone to speak with grace and truth.

What would you think if you only had the information available to the other person? How would you want others to communicate with you? Put yourself in their shoes and understand what they may be thinking or feeling. Give the gift of empathy.

Braintrust

Pixar fosters an incredible environment for creativity and discussion. In the book *Creativity, Inc.*, Ed Catmull details Pixar's creative process called Braintrust meetings.[15] These meetings shape and form ideas and drafts of films into well-rounded stories. *Toy Story*, *Inside Out*, and *Wall-E* each went through Braintrust meetings during production where various creatives in the Pixar organization shared honest thoughts and opinions.

A key to Braintrust meetings is candor. Candor is the act of being "unreserved, honest, or showing sincere expression."[16] When an idea, scene, or storyline could be made better, Pixar employees share honest corrections to help the director improve the film. An environment like Pixar's Braintrust is difficult to create in an instant; openness takes time to weave into the culture of a team or company.

At Pixar, trust is strong enough that movie directors take criticism from any and all individuals who take the time to listen to drafts and watch previews. Egos remain on the sideline as directors understand they can learn from anyone. If you take your work personally, the environment can create friction and distrust among team members.

---

[15] Catmull, E., & Wallace, A. (2014). *Creativity, Inc.: Overcoming the unseen forces that stand in the way of true inspiration*. Random House.

[16] Merriam-Webster. (n.d.). *Candor*. Retrieved June 24, 2021, from https://www.merriam-webster.com/dictionary/candor

While a Braintrust meeting may be difficult to imagine yourself in, it is a driving reason why so many Pixar movies are incredibly well received and top box office performers. The ideas are put through a grinder to create something great by the end.

A key to this meeting style is the ability to separate the person from an idea and the consciousness to separate work from individual identity. Pixar makes it clear when you participate in the Braintrust meetings: Do not attack the person in charge. You share ideas about how the movie makes you feel or what felt off in the storyline. All comments are focused on the work, not the shortcomings of the team or director.

Just like creating successful movies, conversations require you to separate the person and his or her actions or behaviors. You may be frustrated with your friend because she ate your food without asking or borrowed a stapler from your desk and did not bring it back. Before launching into a strenuous conversation, silo the frustrating action in your mind. People often think that asking if you like an idea is the same as asking if you like the person who created the idea. These are two separate things, and we have grown up in dialogue where people interpret them as one and the same. You can still like a person while disagreeing with their behavior.

In order to clearly address a conversation, prepare your heart and mind by separating the actions from the person whom you want to talk to. In doing so, you may realize that the other person doesn't frustrate you as much as you thought.

It may just be a specific action that is preventing you from seeing them in a positive light. My mom always told me that just because someone makes a bad decision does not make them a bad person. You may not like someone's action or behavior but that does not mean you must dislike the person.

Remember:

- Words in your head may not make sense to the other person.
- Separate the person and the behavior or action you are critiquing.
- Give the gift of empathy.

Questions to Ask Yourself:

- How would I feel in the other person's position?
- What do my words mean to the other person?
- Is my frustration justified?
- What else could be going on that is affecting the other person?

Scenario:

Your coworker has shown up late for work and morning meetings for the past two weeks. Due to delays in deliverables and interrupted meetings, your group projects fall behind schedule. This hasn't been a trend before, but your coworker has negatively impacted results for the last two weeks. What are you thinking about in this situation?

CHAPTER 5

Assume the Best

I magine you are Mark, a young college guy sitting in your dorm room, and a girl you are interested in, Caitlyn, sends you a text message about a date planned for tomorrow evening. On your first date last weekend, you two connected well and discovered you had a surprising amount in common. Both of you acknowledged how well the first date went and Caitlyn recognized how naturally comfortable she felt around you. The day before your next date, Caitlyn texts you and says an emergency came up and she would not be able to make it to the date tomorrow, but she wants to get together another time.

As the guy in this situation, what would you think in Mark's position? Most of the time his initial reaction would be that Caitlyn is not interested in him and made up the emergency as an excuse to get out of the date. This thought sends

Mark's mind in a spiral by questioning the feelings he has for Caitlyn to the point where he contemplates whether to end the pursuit right there.

He texts his friends and Caitlyn's mutual friends but cannot get any solid advice. Some of his best friends tell him to ghost her while others suggest he reach out to reschedule the date. This back-and-forth results in hours of lost sleep, way too many glimpses at his phone to check for messages, and a solid headache.

All over a text message that says an emergency came up.

What if Mark assumed the best in the situation? Often, this situation results in the guy and girl going in separate directions, but what if he assumed that Caitlyn actually had an emergency? She did mention that she wants to reschedule for another time. Everything was great up until that text message and then Mark questions his entire existence.

Misinterpretation

The struggle with texts or emails is that we can't read the nonverbal communication from the other person. While a message or email may appear to say one thing to you, the intention behind the words may be completely different.

"Let's talk at 5."
"I need to tell you something later."

Whether you receive these messages in a work email or a text message from your friend, there is an obvious lack of clarity on the receiver's behalf. "Let's talk at 5" could mean anything from choosing a location for happy hour to getting fired from your job. Getting "I need to tell you something later" from your significant other could be a raise at work to an argument about how he/she needs to feel more appreciated in the relationship. If you are lucky, you get the "Nothing bad, don't worry" added to the end.

As the receiver of a message with an ambiguous interpretation, your mind runs through a number of scenarios about what the other person may mean. You mentally prepare to both fight a war and celebrate a massive victory all because of a few words. Rather than throwing yourself through a roller coaster of emotions, assume the other person has the best intentions at heart.

In college and early in my career, I would think through every scenario about what a message could mean. I would question what the other person had to say while hardly ever guessing correctly. Instead of racking my brain for what I did wrong or what could be wrong, I found that assuming the best of the situation keeps me in a positive state of mind, more relaxed, and helps me focus on what is in front of me. On top of an improved mental state, most conversations are not about something bad anyway! We waste precious amounts of energy, focus, and time thinking about the worst possible scenario that never happens because of a simple misinterpretation of words.

When my boss messages or emails me to give him a call, I assume it is to talk about a project coming up that he needs help with. I don't assume I'm getting yelled at for messing up on a deliverable. If a friend texts me and says he wants to talk, I assume it is just to catch up because we have not talked in a while.

You can only control how you react in a situation. The words sent to you or the choices made by another person do not have to affect your demeanor and attitude. If someone chooses to lie to you, that is something they have to live with. You can assume the best and save yourself countless hours of stress and worry.

Group Projects

Unless you are the slacker, everyone dreads most group projects in school. Group projects turn into one or two people pulling the entire weight of the group while the others become experts in twiddling their thumbs. Rarely, you end up in a group of friends who work hard and create ideas that push your group to the next level.

In group projects, we love when people get their work done quickly and accurately. When groupmates don't meet deadlines or deliver their share later than wanted, we get annoyed and frustrated. I fell into the trap of assuming people were just playing video games or wasting time while I sat in the library until midnight multiple nights in a row. I learned I do not know what someone else does every night and it is not fair of me to assume their behavior. During one group project, I was frustrated with one person for not giving me his portion of a paper by the group deadline. Once he finally sent me his share, he explained that he had been on a road trip for baseball and couldn't get it in when I asked. He didn't waste time, I was just impatient.

It took me too long to realize that other people try their best. They do not purposefully let you down or waste time. People have jobs and lives and wouldn't do anything to intentionally let the team down.

If you are a student, how would you approach a group project differently if you assumed your classmates try their best?

Heart Check

2020 was my year of audiobooks. Since Spotify Wrapped told me I listen to four to five hours of music every day, I decided to start making some of that time a little more productive. One of the books that I read/listened to early in 2020 was *Dare to Lead* by Brene Brown.[17] Brene is a leading author and researcher on vulnerability and leadership.

There are numerous great practices for leaders outlined in the book, but one that stood out to me revolves around assuming the best. We each have people that frustrate us or annoy us. Think about that one person who always seems to get on your nerves. It seems like that person always goes out

---

[17]   Brown, B. (2018). *Dare to lead: Brave work. Tough conversations. Whole hearts.* VERMILION.

of his or her way to make your life miserable. This individual may be the person who does not do anything right at work or that teammate who constantly gets under your skin.

What if we assumed that person was trying their best? They probably are. They do not intentionally go out of their way to underperform or frustrate you. How would you interact with, lead, or guide them?

When faced with these questions for the first time, I needed a heart check. There are people who annoy me and I hardly ever take the time to realize they are trying their best. It gave me a new way to look at their actions and behaviors. When we evaluate ourselves, we filter our thoughts based on our best intentions, but we judge others based on the results of their actions. We often recognize that we give our best effort, but we do not give that same benefit of the doubt to others. It is humbling to realize that someone you dislike has goals and dreams of his or her own and none of them revolve around ticking you off.

I shared this concept of assuming the best on my weekly blog, and it is the post I consistently hear about from my readers. Every couple of months, one of my friends shares how she has to remind herself that her classmates or coworkers are trying their best. It is a game-changer mentality that will help you prepare your heart for a conversation with someone else.

Before a difficult conversation, take some time to show grace to the people who annoy you. Prepare your heart for the conversation by knowing the other person is trying their best. How would you approach a conversation differently if you believed the best in others?

Remember:

- Others have dreams and goals that do not revolve around frustrating you.
- Others are trying their best.
- We evaluate ourselves by best intentions, but we judge others based on the results of their actions.

Questions to Ask Yourself:

- How would I respond if I knew this person was trying their best?
- Am I holding this person to a fair standard?

Scenario:

You are a musician recording a single with a live band and audio for a music video. You have been making music for the last five years and consider yourself to be strong musically. One of the guitarists has played guitar for 15 years but has only played for personal enjoyment and to lead worship nights every once in a while. As you are recording the track, the guitarist keeps making small errors that throw off the song, causing the group to record the video over and over again.

You are frustrated with the other person but don't know how to respond. How would you approach this situation?

CHAPTER 6

Learn About the Other Person

H ave you ever played the game where you guess the story of other people you have never met? You and your friends look around and guess the story of another group of friends or couples. My favorite place to do this is at a restaurant, and the best scenario is watching a random couple a few tables away to guess their story.

Imagine a young man and woman in their early 20's sitting at a table together. The man's leg keeps fidgeting up and down while he rubs his palms against his jeans. The woman keeps looking down while keeping her hands between her legs. Based on these observations, you may guess that the two are on their first date. You may make assumptions about where they met or if they connected on a certain dating app.

Friends take turns guessing how many dates they have been on, how many years they have been together, or if they are just friends. While it is purely a guess, you make assumptions about the other people around you. You build up a narrative in your head that is solely based on the outward appearance of others.

You do not want to play the guessing game when approaching a difficult conversation with someone else. A difficult conversation is not a chance for you to make something up or go in blind thinking you will come up with the right answer. You need to get to know the other person in order to host a dialogue that will enact some sort of change or emotion.

Personality Tests

For a long time, I was not a fan of personality tests. I hated being put in a box and being told that I would never change from the type I was labeled. I participated in a mock interview at the beginning of college, and some type of non-traditional personality test was part of the evaluation process. As we walked through my personality, I was told by the assessor what I was not likely to do and which skills I lacked.

While the assessment left me disappointed and in a mental fog, personality tests only provide a picture to understand yourself or others. Personality tests are a snapshot in time based on certain criteria to identify you as an individual.

You are not confined to the exact results of a test, and you can fluctuate between types, especially at a younger age.

Before you enter a conversation, it helps to know the personality type of the person you approach. During the first few weeks of my banking training program, the 23 of us took an in-depth Meyers Briggs personality test. As we discussed each of our personality types, we went around the room and talked about how our types fit into our relationships in the workplace.

Meyer's Briggs categorizes you into four areas:

- Extraversion/Introversion (E/I)
- Sensing/Intuition (S/N)
- Thinking/Feeling (T/F)
- Judging/Perceiving (J/P)

In a study by the University of Prince Edward Island, researchers analyzed the tendencies of an individual's approach to conflict based on one's Meyers Briggs' personality type and the Thomas Killman Conflict Mode Instrument.[18]

There are five main tendencies or approaches to conflict identified in the Thomas Killman Conflict Mode Instrument: competing, accommodating, avoiding, collaborating, and compromising. In their research, they discovered trends in

---

[18]   Percival, T. Q., Smitheram, V., & Kelly, M. (1992). Myers-Briggs type indicator and conflict-handling intention: An interactive approach. *Journal of Psychological Type, 23*, 10–16. https://www.capt.org/jpt/pdfFiles/Percival_T_et_al_Vol_23_10_16.pdf

the Extraversion/Introversion and Thinking/Feeling person-alities and natural approaches to conflict.

Thinking/Feeling

- T's were more likely to be competitive.
- F's were more likely to accommodate and showed a higher tendency towards collaboration.

Extraversion/Introversion

- E's were more likely to compete or collaborate.
- I's were more likely to accommodate or avoid.

I fluctuate between an ISFJ and ISTJ when I take the Meyers Briggs assessment. I know as an introvert my natural tendency is to avoid conflict. Since I am in between T and F, I am naturally competitive in most aspects of life, but I prefer to collaborate in communication. Because I am hyper-aware of my tendencies, I consciously become more assertive when I need to be and address conflict when I want to avoid it.

Learning someone's personality type helps you communicate effectively with how that person feels comfortable. If someone is a natural avoider of conflict, you want to make him/her feel safe and give the floor to honestly share ideas. If someone is assertive, you can be quicker and more decisive because they may like to communicate quickly without wasting time.

Enneagram

The Enneagram is my favorite personality test. *The Road Back to You* by Ian Chron is a great book outlining the Enneagram and details of each type. Rather than 16 different personality types with Meyers Briggs, the Enneagram has 9 personality types. Instead of feeling stuck, each type has healthiness levels as well as a wing-type that you relate to. For myself and others, the Enneagram fits and relates better to individuals than other personality types.

To learn your Enneagram type, you can search for Enneagram personality tests online or read *The Road Back to You* by Ian Chron.

Each type handles conflict differently:[19] [20]

Type 1 (The Perfectionist): Ones can be short-tempered and judgmental with strong opinions. They are assertive and logical when facing conflict.

Type 2 (The Helper): Twos do not want to be taken for granted and can be upset when their contributions are unnoticed. They fear that conflict could hurt the relationship

---

[19] Cohen, M. C. (2007). *Applications of the Enneagram to psychological assessment*. Enneagram.com. http://citeseerx.ist.psu.edu/viewdoc/download?doi=10.1.1.631.2735&rep=rep1&type=pdf

[20] The Enneagram in Business. (n.d.). *Conflict*. Retrieved June 24, 2021, from https://theenneagraminbusiness.com/business-applications/conflict/

between themselves and the other person. Twos are very empathetic and feel the pain and perspectives of others.

Type 3 (The Achiever): Threes attempt to avoid conflict and want to be seen as highly successful but can get angry when upset with another person. They are great at problem-solving and take practical steps towards the future.

Type 4 (The Romantic): Fours can accuse others and get angry and emotional if conflict involves them. When conversations and conflict are real and non-accusing, they can listen for extended periods of time.

Type 5 (The Investigator): Fives will withdraw and hide concerns to avoid conflict. They are extremely logical and solve issues with self-reflection.

Type 6 (The Loyalist): Sixes are anxious around conflict and can create it by challenging motives or actions. They possess a deep desire to resolve conflict and handle feelings and facts fairly and honestly.

Type 7 (The Enthusiast): Sevens avoid conflict and try to avoid tough conversations with jokes or by changing the subject. They are great at bringing new perspectives and points of view to a challenge.

Type 8 (The Challenger): Eights address conflict head-on and take the necessary steps to resolve an issue. They will back-up those who are loyal to them. Eights can be seen as aggressive or make others feel intimidated in tough conversations.

Type 9 (The Peacemaker): Nines are great at listening and mediating a conversation between others. They try to avoid conflict and suppress feelings and opinions to keep a relationship intact.

Chase, my college roommate and best friend, is an 8 on the Enneagram. He invites and approaches conflict. It doesn't scare him to get into a disagreement or debate because a disagreement forces you to show what you know and prove that your argument is valid. On the other hand, most of my family members are Enneagram 9s. 9s typically do not seek out conflict because any disagreement could be seen as something that could hurt the relationship.

Spending time with my family and Chase developed me into someone who is gracious in conflict but also sees the importance of standing up for himself. Knowing the personality type of the person you interact with is key to understanding how to direct a specific conversation, but spending time with other types of personalities develops you into a well-rounded conversationalist. Utilize the Enneagram, Meyers Briggs, Thomas Killman Conflict Mode Instrument, and other personality types to gain insight into how to interact with someone else. You can find free assessments through simple Internet searches.

Seek Advice

Imagine it is the beginning of a new semester of college. You just finished up your advising meeting with your academic counselor or one of your professors. Now that you know which classes to take, you quickly whip open your computer and start scouting out the courses, times, and professors. As you scavenge through the information with a fine-toothed comb, you make notes of different professor options.

Once you know who the professors are for your upcoming classes, who do you go to? Your friends who took the class before you. In some situations, you look for the class that will teach you the most, but most will admit that they asked their friends about which professor would be the easiest chance for an A. Your friends may even convince you to take an 8 a.m. course, a major accomplishment, just because the professor is great.

Why do you go to your friends in that situation? They went through it before you and offer proven advice on the best path. They sat in your position and know what it takes to get the job done. Just like you go to people who have been through your classes, it is valuable to go to others for help with a difficult conversation, certainly if they have gone through a similar situation.

Someone else knows how to deal and communicate with the other person. A lot of times you do not have to reinvent the wheel and go into the conversation blind. Swallowing your pride and asking for help from someone who has been in your shoes can be best for each party during a tense dialogue.

You go to your friends in long-term relationships for relationship advice, not your friend who has been single his entire life because he ruins every relationship. You go to someone who is in really good shape or a trainer for health advice, not the one who struggles to get off the couch and never exercises. We go to people with proven results in other areas of life and conversations don't have to be any different.

This past year, I was preparing for a tough conversation I had to have with a peer of mine. As I thought about what needed to be said, I sat down with a couple of people on this person's team and asked for their advice. I asked someone that was previously in my shoes as well as someone who had worked with the person for an extended period of time. They gave me the words and comfort I needed to create a plan of approach that resulted in necessary change. I will share some of their tips and tricks later in the book.

Research shows you likely fear being an outcast after sharing your thoughts and opinions, and I often feel the same doubt. A lie that plays into that fear is the belief that no one else has gone through what is in front of you. Every situation is different and you may not get the specific advice you want, but you likely are not the first person dealing with your situation. You can learn a lot about how to interact with someone from the experiences of others.

While asking for advice before conversations is great, you cannot solely rely on others to give you advice on every person or situation. Eventually, you must learn how to interact with people by spending time with them. Some people prefer getting to the point quickly while others want to chat it up for 25 minutes of a 30-minute meeting. Some people prefer email while others want you to give them a quick call.

You can't expect to know everyone's style by talking to them for a total of five minutes in a month. The more you communicate and build a relationship, the better you will know how to interact with someone else. You learn how direct they want information. You know who needs gentle wording and who likes direct, blunt feedback.

Go to a happy hour with your coworkers, play a sport with a college classmate in the rec center, or eat a meal with someone you want to get to know. Spend time with others in and out of your typical interactions to get to know them. The more time you spend with someone, the better you will handle a tough conversation.

Remember:

- Learn your and other's personality types to better communicate. Examples include Meyers Briggs (MBTI), Enneagram, Thomas Kilmann Conflict Mode Instrument.
- Spend time with others to learn how they communicate.
- Take advice from someone who has been in your shoes.

Questions to Ask Yourself:

- What do others say about communicating with this person?
- Does this person like direct or gentle feedback?

Scenario:

You have been in an analyst role for the last year at your company and you noticed that whenever you bring up a new idea or proposal it is ignored by others in the room. You want your ideas to be considered and taken seriously. How do you approach the situation?

Step 3
PREPARE THE ENVIRONMENT
— — —

Set the correct stage for the conversation.

CHAPTER 7

One-on-One

During my senior year of college, there was an absurd amount of drama and conflict on my cross country and track team. We dealt with an unexpected coaching change during the summer before my senior year that threw the team into complete limbo.

Even though I didn't run the entire year because of injuries, I was surrounded by the drama and conflict on a daily basis. The team environment was great at the beginning of the year because the men were running and competing well, but it took a turn for the worse when race times and performances began to suffer halfway through cross country season.

During both cross country and track season, our team conversations revolved around common enemies. For most of your friends, you probably have a lot in common and enjoy conversations about those shared interests. For other friends or coworkers, you may only have a basis for conversation because of a common enemy. A common enemy can easily create conversation and bonding between you and another person, but that person or persons can dominate your mind and conversations if you aren't careful.

While my team had strong friendships that still continue past college, our team fell into the pattern of only talking about our common enemies. The year was filled with complaining and frustration because of our team situation and environment.

Through all of the drama, there were conversations and action happening behind the scenes that caused some issues later on during the year. Some people had inside information while others were left out, for their benefit.

Towards the end of the school year, the team was divided so we held an athlete-only meeting to level the playing field and get everyone on the same page. As the guys talked, we shared some things happening behind the scenes and talked about how we could move forward together. During the meeting, a teammate (let's call him Joe) spoke up and called out another guy (let's call him Brandon) who wasn't in the meeting. Joe brought up things that Brandon had done recently and said that he didn't have a team-first mentality. Joe specifically called out this teammate, Brandon, who could not defend himself.

Because Brandon was not there to speak up for himself, I responded by using Joe's own logic against him and shared some things that I was upset with about his behavior throughout the year. While I remained absolutely calm and controlled my voice, I was direct and blunt.

I embarrassed Joe in front of his teammates and best friends. While some of the comments I made needed to be said, I did not handle the opportunity correctly. I put Joe in a vulnerable position by criticizing him in front of others. It made him rightfully frustrated, upset, and emotional. While we eventually sat down and had a conversation, the sting of that moment will probably never go away for him, and that is my fault. I did not consider how it would feel to be in his position.

There is an old phrase, "Praise publicly and criticize privately." I ignored that major piece of leadership in that moment. Most leadership and management textbooks talk about the necessity to privately give constructive criticism. People are more comfortable and receptive to a message if it is done one-on-one instead of in front of a big group. Instead of a person thinking about how he or she is being perceived in front of others, they can focus on the conversation at hand. When you challenge someone else's credibility in front of others, they go into defense mode instead of remaining open to what you are trying to say.

As you approach a difficult conversation in your life, consider the environment in which you are presenting certain feedback and criticism. The same message presented one-on-one can impact someone more than a different environment.

Direct Conversations

You know the sports parents. The ones who believe their child is entitled to playing time and deserves to take the game winning shot. The parent who talks about their child non-stop as if he or she is the next LeBron James or Candace Parker.

No matter how over the top your parents are, they should never be the one to talk to your coach about playing time. Every coach hates dealing with the parents of an athlete instead of the athlete directly. Why would your boss feel any different?

In high school, whether you want it or not, parents can intervene if something needs to be done for your well-being. Once you are in college and the working world, your mom cannot call your boss to get you an extra week of vacation or another chance at a special project.

If you have an issue with how you are being treated, your team environment, or anything else related to your job, you have to talk to someone yourself. People do not want to hear about your problems through someone else.

During a bout of communication issues on our athletic team, Captain Jake Poyner taught us the importance of going to a person directly with an issue. "When you have an issue with something someone else did or something they said, you need to go to them directly with your issue. That face-to-face confrontation and conversation, while scary and sometimes acutely frustrating, will always result in better and stronger friendships, team community, and reciprocal respect for each other. It's difficult to do this, but if we all do this for each other, we become better, more thoughtful, more loving, more wise, and more mature."

Gossip is a tool of the incompetent and a voice used when one feels insecure. When you go to someone directly, you show that you respect the other person enough to have a conversation in person. You know the people who go behind backs to get something they want. While a person may be seeking personal gain, they may simply go behind someone's back because they don't feel physically or emotionally safe holding a conversation.

Safety is a major part of a one-on-one conversation. If you don't feel safe or comfortable approaching a conversation because of fear for your personal wellbeing, physical, emotional, or mental, then seek assistance in approaching a difficult conversation. Go to someone you can trust who can help take the necessary steps forward.

Avoiding a conversation that you know you can have, or going behind someone's back for your own personal gain, will lead to larger relational issues.

Even adults who have been in the workplace for decades still struggle to go to someone directly with an issue. At the beginning of the year, I heard multiple stories about coworkers who went to another person's boss instead of going to the person first. It is amazing how age does not necessarily mean someone will handle conflict or tension appropriately. You will set yourself apart and stand out as a young professional if you handle issues or concerns directly with someone instead of needing a boss to intervene.

Varying Scenarios

Jon Gordon says, "Where there is a void in communication, negativity will fill it."[21] Going to someone directly eliminates the "he said, she said" game. You will get to share exactly what you want to say and hear exactly what someone has for you. Ambiguity causes drama and confusion, and the easiest way to limit that is by sitting down and having a one-on-one conversation with another human being.

Consider the following guidelines when deciding between approaching a conversation in a group or privately.

When to approach one-on-one:

- A personal matter between you and another person
- Specific feedback on a project or constructive criticism

When to approach in a group:

- A team feedback session
- Criticism and open communication are clearly invited in a group setting

---

[21] Gordon, J. (2018). *The power of a positive team: Proven principles and practices that make great teams great (Jon Gordon).* Wiley.

Your default for a conversation should be to go to someone directly, in private. If someone else invites feedback in an open space, then share with others. Think about the content being shared and how you would want to have it received.

Just like how you shouldn't break up with someone over a text message, it is best to have someone hear your issues from you, not from another coworker, teammate, or your mom.

Heads Up

The great thing about having a twin is that you never have to do anything alone growing up. I had someone who would play basketball against me and a friend to go on bike rides or runs. When I was about four or five years old, my twin brother and I were playing tag in the backyard. Our yard was nice and spread out besides one thing—the trampoline. I was always the faster twin growing up, so my brother tried to catch me while I dodged his encounters. As I channeled my inner Usain Bolt, I sped away from my brother's outstretched hands and looked back to see where my predator stood. While I peered backwards, I neglected to pay attention to the location of the giant trampoline in the middle of our yard. At that age, I was a perfect height where my forehead was right in line with the massive, circular metal pipe holding the stretched trampoline. Before I knew it, I was seeing stars as my brother tagged me and yelled, "You're it!"

People don't want to be clothes lined by a conversation. They do not want to be smacked across the face with a conversation that comes out of nowhere. If you have something specific that you want to talk to your coach, boss, or friend about, it is often best to give them notice ahead of time. You want them to have something to contribute to the conversation rather than frozen by shock or surprise.

If you have an issue to work out, then give some preface of the situation to the other person. If you want to talk about your hours in the office, then say you want to talk about your hours. If you want to talk about the team environment, then give a heads up. You do not have to give many details, but a nice overview of what you want to address can help a conversation move in the right direction.

Some conversations are best to be held in an instant, so be able to interpret the difference. Early in college, I was upset with one of my friends so I texted her that we needed to talk soon. I sent the dreaded, "We need to talk" text that scares anyone out of their shoes. I knew that she was busy for the next couple of days, so I told her we could talk after the weekend finished.

My text sent her into such a whirlwind that she ended up calling me right then. Certain conversations do not need much of a preface nor should they have a week's build up. You do not want to be sitting on hold with customer service for a week just to get a bad comment sorted out. Sometimes a heads up can be counterproductive to the end goal you are trying to accomplish. If a heads up is just going to misinterpret your message, then give a heads up 5 to 10 minutes ahead of a conversation and get it over with.

Remember:

- If you have an issue with something someone is doing, go to them directly.
- Publicly praise, privately criticize.

Questions to Ask Yourself:

- Have I talked to the person directly?
- Is this the right environment to hold this conversation?
- Should I give this person a heads up?

Scenario:

You are a collegiate volleyball player. Before practice, your team does different activation exercises and a little bit of jogging to prepare for the intensity of practice. The entire team is supposed to do the warm-up exercises together, but one teammate always puts in her headphones and does the exercises to the side by herself. You and your teammates are frustrated that she isn't joining the group and your coach isn't paying attention to the warm-up most days because she is preparing for practice. How do you approach the situation?

CHAPTER 8

Raise the Green Flag

A few years ago, my family and I were on the beach for Spring Break. On an afternoon walk, we noticed a panicked family on the edge of the water. As we scanned the area to see what was happening, we noticed that someone was stuck in the ocean. A man swam towards the beach but was stuck in the powerful current and could not make his way back to the safety of the sand.

As the man struggled, a lifeguard out of nowhere shot across the beach like a bolt of lightning and dove under the waves with a life preserver dragging behind him. After a struggle and pull, the lifeguard successfully returned the drowning man to the safety of the beach with his family.

Once we knew the man was alright, we made our way back to our section of the beach and noticed the color of the flag: yellow. If you have ever been to the beach then you are familiar with the different colored flags and their meanings. If the flag is red, that means the water is highly hazardous and you should not enter the ocean. If the flag is yellow, that means it is a medium hazardous day and you must take caution when swimming in the water. A green flag means low hazard and it is safe to enjoy the ocean.

The weather conditions greatly impact the amount of caution and enjoyment you have at the beach. If lifeguards fly the green flag, you are good to jump in the waves and do not even think twice about anything bad happening. If lifeguards fly a red flag, you keep your distance from the water because you don't want to be the next horror story. Calm water makes you calm and excited. Dangerous water creates a sense of fear.

The environment you create in a conversation is similar to that of the beach. You are raising a green, yellow, or red flag during every conversation. You send a signal to the other person about how much caution they should take when approaching you.

Which color flag are you flying? Do you fly the green flag, which invites others to join you, or do you fly the red flag, which scares others away? You control the weather. You can make people feel comfortable in a conversation or force them away. Your presence and emotion dictate the interactions that others have with you.

Nonverbal Communication

You may guess that your words have a large impact on how your message is received by another person, but when people try to read you, they look at your body language.

Leanne Smith, a Lipscomb University professor and business communication specialist, taught me throughout college that 55% of meaning comes from non-verbal cues, 38% is from tone, and 7% is from the actual words you say.[22] [23] No matter how perfect your words are, you can still give a drastically different message than what you intend.

Your posture speaks volumes to the person across from you. According to an *Entrepreneur* article, "The position of your body can communicate a lot about what you're thinking or feeling. If your body posture is 'closed,' such as when your arms are folded or your head is down, people will think you're not interested in having a conversation. If your posture is "open," however, with your shoulders back and your head up, you'll be seen as welcoming and friendly."[24]

---

[22] Smith, L. W. (n.d.). *Delivery*. Leanne W. Smith. Retrieved June 24, 2021, from https://www.leannewsmith.com/delivery

[23] Thompson, J. (2011, September 30). *Is nonverbal communication a numbers game?* Psychology Today. https://www.psychologytoday.com/us/blog/beyond-words/201109/is-nonverbal-communication-numbers-game

[24] Entrepreneur. (2017, August 7). *7 body-language hacks to try when meeting new people.* https://www.entrepreneur.com/article/298254#:%7E:text=If%20you%20want%20to%20ask,be%20reserved%20with%20your%20gestures.

Additionally, if you give a compliment to someone, but you are looking at your feet and are mumbling, you will give the impression that you don't mean any of your words.

In *The Communications Guys Podcast*, Joe Navarro highlighted an interesting fact about body language. Navarro was a former FBI agent and is recognized as an expert in nonverbal communication. Of various nonverbal cues, the face is the most dishonest part of the body. People are great at controlling their face, but Joe shared that the feet are the most honest part of the body. Feet will shake, move, or even point towards the door subconsciously.[25]

People will give you nonverbal hints of how they feel around you. Be aware of them and adjust your body language to make others feel comfortable. If someone is fidgeting their feet or looking at the door, try to make them feel more comfortable.

Be the type of person others want to interact with. If you want someone to yell and target your insecurities, then yell and target someone's weaknesses. If you want someone to respect you and care about you, then respect and care about someone else. You are inclined to react how others react. If someone is heated and emotional but you remain calm and composed, you show wisdom and respect.

---

[25]   Barret, T., & Downs, T. (Hosts). (2019, December 2). Dealing with conflicts before they become conflicts (No. 169) [Audio podcast episode]. In *The Communications Guys Podcast*. Spotify. https://open.spotify.com/episode/4N2Hvu3l6s3fChVihWDqOu?si=b3f0b680f5fa4e89

One of my favorite quotes is, "The person you have to be most worried about is the calmest person in the room." The calmest person in a room is able to think on his or her toes. She can listen to the points of others without being caught up in what she has to say. He can keep the conversation about the task at hand instead of making it a battle of emotions.

One thing that turns a conversation for the worst is over-the-top yelling. Do not use yelling as a crutch to support your argument. Emotions are real and should be expressed, but do not try to coerce someone into a decision by exerting dominance with your voice.

Yelling, when used effectively, is a method used when there is too much noise for others to hear your message. When you have a one-on-one meeting, there should not be noise disrupting the conversation. Choose a place free of distractions to avoid the need to yell over large crowds or background noise. You can be stern without letting your emotions take over when you are upset.

Have you ever been somewhere in your house and heard a family member, probably your dad, scream from the living room? Instead of something being wrong, he is just yelling about how his favorite sports team made the "dumbest mistake possible" like J. R. Smith in the NBA Finals. He sits in his recliner and screams at the black box across the room as if the players on the court or field can actually hear him.

When you are in a conversation with someone else, you are not separated by the TV screen. The other person can actually hear you if you are yelling. Your emotions factor into the message being delivered to someone else because tone is 38% of your message.

A common phrase in golf is "drive for show, putt for dough." If you want to be a flashy golfer then you break out the largest club in your bag and swing as hard as possible. Even if you can drive the ball really far and straight, it does not mean the hole is over. You must hit iron shots, chips, and putts to eventually get your golf ball in the hole.

Even if you can drive it straight, putting is where you make your money. You spend more strokes around the green than you do on the tee box. If you cannot putt very well, then your flashy drives don't do you any good.

Think of yelling as hitting the driver and putting as a personal, controlled conversation. Yelling will gather the attention of others and it may make you look powerful and commanding, but at the end of the day, it does not get your message across effectively. The best communicators have clear messages that others understand, not loud and flashy billboards.

Remember:

- Your emotions control the room.
- Nonverbal communication accounts for 93% of your message.

Questions to Ask Yourself:

- Am I creating an environment where others feel comfortable having conversations with me?
- Am I keeping my emotions in control?
- Am I giving the other person my full attention?

Scenario:

You manage a team of 10 employees and one of your teammates walks over to your office to talk. The person knocks on the open door and says your name to get your attention. Instead of turning around on the knock, you keep looking at your computer for an extra 5 to 10 seconds before acknowledging the person in your office. Eventually, you turn around distracted and appear slightly annoyed that someone is disrupting you.

How would you react differently in this scenario? What little things could you do to make your employee feel comfortable?

CHAPTER 9

Situations

Every situation in life differs. Certain situations require various methods of response. This chapter addresses common environments and situations for students and young professionals.

School

During my freshman year of college, I took a macroeconomics course as one of my business requirements. Every week we read a chapter out of a book and wrote responses to a list of questions for an online forum. Before the forum was opened to discuss with other students, we received a grade on our original responses.

One week during the middle of the semester, I checked Blackboard for my grade and was shocked to see a 0/90. My professor's reasoning for the first and only zero of my college career was that my responses were generic and did not reflect that I had read the chapter. I was fuming for the rest of the day because I read and understood the chapter! After I regained my composure the next day, I acknowledged that I had not given my best work, but I felt it was at least good enough to receive some points.

Instead of talking to my professor, I vented to my friends. For a couple of days, I was one of those students who would complain about the bad grade as if it were the professor's fault. Since it was early in the semester, it dropped my grade to a C, so I knew it would be an uphill battle to bring it back up to the high expectations I set for myself. I was so determined that I did not miss a single point for the rest of the semester outside of a couple points on the final.

While I ended up getting an A in the course, the situation could have been handled much better on my end. I now know that my professor is easy to approach and have a conversation with and I had no reason to be scared of getting my feelings hurt. I ended up taking five of his classes and he is my favorite professor from college.

What most students do not realize is that professors want you to come to talk to them and ask questions. They do not teach so you just sit in class, leave, and take tests. Professors teach because they want to develop relationships, mentor, and help you reach your goals. They are not out to get you by giving poor grades.

When you talk to professors about topics covered in class or about a homework assignment, you show that you are interested in the material and care about learning. Professors are willing to have conversations with you if you are concerned about your grade or think there may have been a mix up. I know I am not the only one who received a below-average grade that left me frustrated for days.

Instead of fuming for weeks, or the rest of the semester, it helps to approach a professor from a place of wanting to understand. Go to them in their office, after class, or the local coffee shop. Approach the conversation from a place where you want to understand more about a grade you received. Ask for the rationale behind the grade and what could have been done to make it better. Do not approach the conversation by trying to prove a point or make them out as a villain. Go to understand and adjust as the conversation progresses. You may be in the wrong more than you think.

Group Projects

Another common area for difficult conversations in school is group projects. Some group projects are the perfect combination of skills and abilities, but most are not. In my experience, group projects in the workplace are effective because there are multiple perspectives collaborating and creating new, better ideas. In college, however, it was often the opposite. Group projects were a random assortment of students but frequently resulted in one or two students putting the team on their backs.

It's tough to hold classmates accountable you barely know, but you can take these steps to help your team be successful on the front end.

- Set group expectations.
- Determine talents and goals.
- Ask what could have been better.

As you enter upper-level courses, there is a greater chance that you get assigned a group for the entire semester. In my capstone business course, we chose groups that lasted. We completed weekly assignments together, but we also had presentations or projects throughout the semester.

Over ten weeks, we competed against other groups in the class in a business simulation. We each ran an international footwear company and made pricing, marketing, sales, and production decisions to maximize profits. Every week, the scoreboard was updated to show whose company of the eight had the greatest profit and revenue.

Everyone in my group was extremely competitive, and we ended up winning seven out of the ten individual weeks and remained atop the leaderboard from week two of the competition through the end of the simulation. Besides the natural drive to succeed, my group did a few great things to set us up for success. We set weekly meetings outside of class to get together and review our company strategy, the strengths of each teammate were identified and positioned to help our team maximize effectiveness, and we level-set in the middle of the semester to ask what we could be doing better as a group to make everyone feel comfortable and confident.

The frequent meetings allowed for consistent feedback and ideas to make our team and strategy better. When we did a deeper conversation halfway through the semester, we found that a team member was not as knowledgeable on the areas that others had been working on in the simulation, so we adjusted to make her feel more involved in the bigger picture. When you ask for feedback in advance, you become more approachable for others.

In most classes, you will be assigned to a group for one project and then move on. In those situations, take the time to sit down with your team to outline your strategy. When you set expectations at the beginning of the project, you can hold others accountable if they are not meeting that predetermined standard. It makes it easier to tell someone they are not pulling their weight if you collectively decide on a plan of action. Set the expectation early to make a difficult conversation easier if it is needed.

Tough conversations with professors or classmates do not have to be scary or taboo. Professors want to have a conversation with you and are not out to get you. Your group projects can fly by with greater ease when you set expectations on the front end.

Athletics

The Last Dance took the world by storm in early 2020. The unseen footage of the 1997–98 Chicago Bulls brought millions of people behind the scenes of one of the greatest NBA teams of all time. Young adults saw sides and stories about Michael Jordan that we had only heard from parents or grandparents. The drama, last-second shots, and pure greatness captivated America and the world for five weeks straight.

Even though the documentary was incredibly well-received by viewers, there remains some controversy over Michael Jordan's leadership style. He is portrayed as someone who would do anything to achieve greatness. He pushed his teammates to extreme levels where there were often fights during practice. Steve Kerr, now coach of the Golden State Warriors, describes a time in practice where he and MJ got heated and Michael punched him in the face.

Jordan claims that his style of leadership and work ethic comes from the desire to want something that other people do not understand. He never asked his teammates to do something he would not do himself.

While Jordan's style and communication aren't the best approach for most of us, it shows that athletics can be different than other areas of life. Being on the practice field, court, or track is different than sitting in an office or classroom. Tempers fly and yelling is common to push athletes to be their best.

There will be disagreements between you and your coaches when you spend multiple hours together every day. You will have times where you disagree with a workout or training philosophy. You will have scheduling conflicts with a practice or accidentally sleep through a morning weights session.

You will have aches, pains, and injuries that your coaches or athletic trainers may not believe or understand.

At the end of the day, you know your body. When you do not feel like certain training is working for you, you need to have a conversation. If you want to make some adjustments because your body is breaking down, your coach needs to know.

What you will realize is that your coaches, if they know what they're doing, have reasons for why they implement a certain type of training at a specific point in the season. A lot of times you will not learn the details until you go and sit down with them.

I had multiple hip surgeries during my collegiate running career. As my senior year started up, I was slowly getting back into running and I sat down with my coach to talk about my plan for the season. I went out of my way to have a meeting with him because I knew that I needed training adjustments for my frail body.

In our meeting, we agreed to cut a hard, tempo workout out of my weekly training and cross-train multiple days each week. I would not have gotten that path unless I sat down and had a conversation around what was best for my body.

During the team meeting mentioned earlier in the book, a major point of contention revolved around the training plan. Both men and women on the team often felt tired from the weekly intensity that led to sluggish races and workouts during the middle of the season. Our coach acknowledged the concerns by saying that he has always had athletes complain about feeling fatigued during the middle of the season. If athletes did not feel fatigued, he would be concerned. He showed that the same concerns had been felt before and explained some of the reasoning behind the training plan.

Whether it was a good training plan or not, our coach had a reason and plan behind his training and methodology. The coaches of your team, if they are smart, have a plan behind a workout or practice. Do not be afraid to ask them about your concerns or share how your body feels.

The coach's job is to push you, not to be your cheerleader. You may not agree with everything your coach is saying, but they also have a responsibility to make you better. A conversation can get you on the same page to help reach your individual and team goals.

Teammate Conflict

Outside of coaching, conflict among team members is necessary to become successful. Jon Gordon shared that one of the keys to a great team is having healthy conflict.[26] He says the best teams do not shy away from holding each other accountable and push each other to become great. Michael Jordan in *The Last Dance* is a perfect example of that approach.

---

[26] PURPOSE ON TAP. (2020, April 14). *Purpose on tap | JON GORDON | 04.08.20* [Video]. YouTube. https://www.youtube.com/watch?v=v0NEuphWcT0

In my freshmen year of college, our cross country and track team brought in 16 freshmen. We joined as a massive class that would transform the team over the next four years. Our recruiting class consisted of some phenomenal athletes, but we didn't perform up to the hype our first indoor track season.

Our class got together and held a freshmen-only meeting where we called each other out for not racing to our capability. While it is not easy to tell your team that you are falling behind expectations, it can serve as a fire to ignite work ethic and performance when used properly. The following weekend, the men ran multiple personal records (PR's in the running world) because of the new-found motivation.

In athletics, that strong-willed approach can work better than in the workplace. Athletes are used to being ridden hard and pushed on a daily basis by coaches and teammates. Every athletic team shares a common goal, often that of winning a championship. Do not be afraid to call out a teammate in practice or sit down and have a conversation afterward. The conflict is an attempt to make the team better to reach that clear, shared goal.

Some people can handle criticism and coaching differently than others. You spend a lot of time with your teammates and know how each like to be pushed. Some people want to be called out in front of the group while others prefer a gentler, personal conversation. Tailor your feedback for each person on a team.

Conflict is a necessary part of any team when you spend countless hours together. Embrace the disagreements and work together to win games, matches, races, and championships.

Work

If you work a traditional eight-to-five job, you will spend most of your day at the office. You will probably spend more time around your coworkers than any other people in your life. Due to the extended time, it is key to have strong relationships and communication among your work group.

Fostering a positive, connected environment is important for any team to succeed. In a study of business teams, Emily Heaphy and Marcial Losada discovered "the factor that made the greatest difference between the most and least successful teams, was the ratio of positive comments to negative comments that the participants made to one another. The average ratio for the highest-performing teams was 5.6 positive comments to negative."[27] The lowest performing teams only had about one positive comment for every three negative comments.

While a strong positive to negative ratio is key, there must be times where you share concerns or issues with others. In the workplace, that is most commonly called feedback. Some of

[27] Zenger, J., & Folkman, J. (2013, March 15). *The ideal praise-to-criticism ratio*. Harvard Business Review. https://hbr. org/2013/03/the-ideal-praise-to-criticism

the best companies have strong cultures of feedback because it is necessary to evolve and adapt.

If you sit around and do the same work over and over again, you are not getting better. Feedback from others is necessary to make your work better and to elevate the overall performance of your team.

Feedback is not just for a manager to give an employee; it occurs at all levels and stages of the organization. Just because you may not have a certain position does not mean you cannot share your opinions that can help improve your team or company. The best managers do not want a bunch of "Yes Men" telling them everything they do is the best thing since sliced bread. They want employees who will push back on their ideas to make them better.

Growing up, I commonly heard the best way to give feedback is through the feedback sandwich. You start with a positive, insert a constructive comment, and finish with a positive. The goal of this sandwich and structure is to warm someone up and then have them thinking about something positive at the end. I'm not a fan of the feedback sandwich approach because it forces comments that make the positive feedback appear insincere.

The easiest way to share constructive feedback is through constant communication. When you communicate on a regular basis, you make it easier to bring up issues, concerns, or questions as you work. If you only talk with your boss every six months, it is difficult to deal with issues that happened two or three months in the past.

Be Specific

The best way to provide constructive feedback is through specific examples.

Jacqueline works on a branding team for a small company. She and her teammates develop and create marketing materials that impact how the company interacts with customers. She notices a pattern when she sits down with her boss for weekly one-on-ones. Every time her boss gives her instructions, she flies through details she wants Jacqueline to work on for the week. Instead of walking through the items slowly, she throws out project after project without giving Jacqueline time to write down what needs to be completed.

When Jacqueline leaves her boss's office, she never has a complete grasp of her work. This misunderstanding causes Jacqueline to ask her boss questions every day and leads to interruptions and delays on projects.

Ultimately, Jacqueline wants to tell her boss that she wants slower instructions and a better understanding after their one-on-one meetings. Instead of saying, "You need to give me better instructions," here is a great way for Jacqueline to bring up her concerns to her boss in their next meeting:

"I noticed that I leave our meetings without a full understanding of the details of my work every week. For example, last week when I worked on the rebranding of the company logo I didn't catch all of the details that you wanted to be included because we flew through the instructions in 30 seconds. I ended up taking more of your time throughout the week by interrupting you every few hours. Can we do a better job of taking our time through weekly projects so I have a better understanding and I am not interrupting you during the week over things we already discussed?"

This approach brings feedback to Jacqueline's boss's attention and shows a clear example of where this came into play. Instead of just sharing that she wants to go slower through instructions, Jacqueline provided a specific example of how her boss can improve. On top of sharing a real occurrence, the feedback example speaks to how it can directly help her boss through fewer interruptions.

You could tell your boss that you want more work to do or share a different way to run team meetings, but giving feedback is better with specific examples. If you want more projects to work on, come up with examples of things other people are doing that you want to accomplish. If you have a suggestion for the structure of team meetings, share how a specific meeting was an ineffective use of time because there was no preparation on the front end.

The more consistent you are in communication, the easier it is for feedback to raise organically. Be specific when being constructive and come with an idea for how to move forward.

Remember:

- Every situation requires a different response.
- Every person likes feedback in a certain way.
- Your professors, coaches, and bosses want you to bring up concerns.

Questions to Ask Yourself:

- How does my environment shape my response?
- What is a specific example where I can give feedback?

Scenario:

You are in a group project and no one shows up at the decided time. All of a sudden, everyone has something else on their schedules and you are left doing all of the work with a big deadline in a couple of days. How do you talk to your group members and get on the same page for the deadline?

Step 4
PREPARE YOUR WORDS

— — —

Discover the words for your conversation.

CHAPTER 10

Determine Your Goal

n college, I took an exploring nature course as a literature and science combo credit. During the semester, I completed an active assignment in nature and journaled about my experiences. Normally, I would choose to go for a hike and spend hours in the seclusion of a forest. Unfortunately, I tore the labrum in my hip and had surgery scheduled for a couple of weeks later, so I couldn't hike for more than 5 to 10 minutes before my hip started killing me. With my active options limited, I camped overnight in a park in Nashville.

Part of the exercise involved journaling in-depth details of the scene around my mini campsite. The problem with camping at night in the middle of the woods is that I could not see anything. I could not see my own hand in front of my face, and the only way I could navigate my surroundings was from the flashlight on my phone.

Instead of writing an eloquent paper about the beautiful colors of a forest or lake, I somehow connected my pitch-black experience to a human's need for visual stimulation to truly appreciate nature. Needless to say, I did not get much out of the activity. My active nature activity resulted in a poor grade on my paper and bug bites all over my face the next morning. All of which were well deserved.

In the paper, I did mention that I could not go hiking, kayaking, or participate in another activity because of my hip. When I got my grade back, the professor commented in red pen by asking why I had not gone hiking or completed a different style of activity. In my mind, I had missed points because I physically could not complete an active activity.

After class, I went by my professor's office with one goal: understand why I was given a poor grade. Due to some of the comments on my paper, I felt there may have been confusion on the activity I completed.

I sat down in his office and explained, "I'm here to understand the grade I received on my active activity paper. I saw a comment about not completing something more active and I physically cannot because of my hip. I want to see if the fact that my hip limited me factored into my grade."

He explained that he did not realize how bad my hip condition was, but the paper was not well written and did not show a deep enough connection to nature. He offered for me to take it to the other professor teaching the class if I wanted to receive a regrade on the assignment.

I approached that conversation with the goal of understanding my grade and I received an explanation. I did not storm into my professor's office to prove my paper's worth or argue for a higher score. I accepted what he said and did not go to the other professor for the chance at a better grade. For the rest of the year, that professor gave me better grades than he had earlier in the semester. While I could not tell if my writing drastically improved, I believe I earned his grace because I was willing to have a conversation with him and listen to his point of view. I did not go behind his back to get more points and respected his decision.

Set a Goal

Set a goal before every difficult conversation. Know what you want to accomplish before you immerse yourself in the situation. An old saying says, "If you fail to plan, you plan to fail." If you sit down to address some type of conflict and just expect to naturally talk it out, you will walk away with less than expected.

In my conversation with my professor, I sought out an understanding of a grade and I received that answer. If I wanted to argue for an 80% on the paper, I would have given specific points to defend my paper. If you want to talk through roommate difficulties, come ready with specific behaviors you want to adjust to make living better for all of you in your apartment, dorm, or house. If you want to talk to a friend who never Venmos you for meals, set a goal amount of money you want to be repaid during the conversation and a deadline of when you want the rest of your money returned. Your goal influences the words, directness, and intensity you show during a conversation.

During the day, I work as a sales analyst for a large bank. A typical day includes me preparing pitch decks or materials for client meetings. In order to tailor the presentations, I am involved with strategic discussions about how we can add value for clients. Before most client calls, the deal team will have "Pre-calls" to discuss an approach for the meeting the next day.

We sit down and discuss the client's goals and how we fit into those long-term objectives. When the team sits down with the client or logs on to the online meeting, we are all on the same page about what we want to accomplish. The client meetings where we organize internal pre-calls ahead of time result in much smoother conversations and better results for the client and the bank.

If we prepare materials, we do not just walk into a client meeting and sit down for a casual conversation about nothing. There are times to casually catch up with friends, clients, or business partners, but when you have important business conversations, you come prepared.

If you have a difficult conversation with the potential for conflict, you need to have a goal and a plan for your meeting. Preparation is not reserved for meetings with big money on the table or clients. If you want time off for vacation, then come with certain days off in your mind. If you want a break from working late nights, then know the specific time you want to clock out. If you want to race certain distances during the track season, then come ready with the events and meets that you want to run. If you want to get credit for some assignment that was misgraded, then know what to ask for.

There is a difference between asking for a change and asking for something specific. Notice the difference in the situations below.

Situation 1: You ask your boss for fewer hours because you spend too many nights in the office.

Vague request: "Hey boss, can I work fewer hours because I'm starting to feel burnt out?"

Specific request: "Hey boss, can I leave at 4:30 every day next week? I'm starting to feel burnt out."

Situation 2: Your roommate is loud in the morning and wakes you up every day on her way to class. Most mornings, you sit awake for an extra two hours instead of getting needed sleep.

Vague request: "Hey, could you be a little quieter in the morning when you get ready for class?"

Specific request: "Hey, when you bang your drawers and the door in the morning, it usually wakes me up and makes it difficult to fall back asleep. Would you be able to close those quieter in the morning?"

If you do not know the goal of your conversation, here is my suggestion—seek understanding. There is often more going on in a tense situation than you realize. Reality is made up of multiple perspectives, not just your own viewpoint. There are often moving pieces behind the scenes or blind spots for you or the other person. When you approach with a heart of understanding, it is easier for each side to relax, feel comfortable, and make necessary changes.

Listen

You may wonder how to approach a conversation with a heart of understanding. It is simple—listen

There is a difference between listening and hearing. Hearing is just recognizing that a sound hits your ear, but listening requires effort. You must consciously work to understand what sound hits your ear and interpret the information. It is easy to hear because you do not need to process any information, but it is harder to listen.

When you are in a conversation, are you hearing or listening? Do you actually know what the other person is saying or do her words go in one ear and out the other? Think about a typical conversation with coworkers, family, or friends. Do you do all of the talking or is there a balance? Do you find that people know more about you than you know about others?

You will miss opportunities if you always talk. A friend may be going through a tough family divide or a difficult manager change at their job. If you are too busy talking about yourself then you shut off another's ability to open up about their needs. If you do not actually listen to what other people say, you will miss the opportunity to serve those who need you. If you go into a conversation to understand, you will end up learning about another person.

During high school, I would try to sit for five seconds before speaking up in a conversation. I am naturally a listen-first type of person and prefer to let someone talk my ear off if they have things to say. That five-second pause can be the time that someone needs to get something important off their chest.

Years ago, I shared that tip with one of my good friends from high school. She recently reached out to me about how she consistently tries to use that when in a conversation to make sure others feel heard and listened to. Here is what she said:

"I still to this day hear your voice say take a five-second pause when listening to people because that is what they need sometimes to continue a thought. I have used it so much in my life the last two years and it has gotten me to have conversations with people I never would have thought and even helped save a life."

You may have a nemesis who always gets on your nerves. Instead of assuming you will never agree with that person, take the time to listen to him or her. Learn his background, know her interests, and understand how she thinks. Maybe you will change your mind about that individual or a situation. One of my best friends says, "We are more distant than different." Grow closer to them by listening. Decrease that distance and maybe you will see that you are less different than originally thought. You may even help save a life.

Key Phrases:

- "I want to understand _____."
- "Can I (insert specific action and timeframe)?"

Remember:

- Set a specific goal for your conversation.
- If you don't have a goal for the conversation, seek understanding and listen.

Questions to Ask Yourself:

- What is my goal for the conversation?
- What do I not understand about the situation?
- Should I be listening instead of talking?

Scenario:

Your friend and coworker is in a minority group at your company. He does not see many people like him and feels isolated and unwelcome at times. While nothing is intentionally being done to cause the isolation, you notice he has been distant the last couple of weeks and is not sharing ideas in meetings. How do you approach a conversation with your friend?

CHAPTER 11

Clarity

Have you ever seen a newspaper or news channel headline that made zero sense? When you read the headline and could not understand the intent of the story because of how the title was phrased? Here are a few examples:

Headline: *Enraged Cow Injures Farmer with Axe*

Did a cow really stand up on two legs and axe down a farmer? If so, I wouldn't go cow tipping anytime soon.

Headline: *Dealers Will Hear Car Talk at Noon*

I thought cars could only talk in *Transformers*. I need to see this talking car!

Headline: *Milk Drinkers are Turning to Powder*

Now you have an excuse for not drinking your milk. Before you know it, you may turn into a powder as if Thanos snapped his fingers.[28]

Obviously, each of those headlines can be misinterpreted from the author's intent. The farmer was probably holding an axe, car dealers probably have "car talk" on their lunch breaks, and people are switching to protein powder drinks instead of milk. Besides a lack of self-editing, the major piece missing from these news headlines is clarity.

As indicated with the titles above, a message that you understand may convey a completely different meaning to someone else. Clarity is key to properly transfer a message from one person to another.

Communication consists of two endpoints, a sender and receiver. The sender sends a message to the receiver, who then provides feedback to the sender. It would be great if the message were easily translated from one person to another, but unfortunately, the message travels through some type of interference called noise.[29] Noise can disrupt the message or feedback from one point to the other. The noise could be background voices or music surrounding you and another

---

[28]   Just-One-Liners.com. (n.d.). *Headline*. Retrieved June 25, 2021, from https://www.just-one-liners.com/hdlines/headline/

[29]   Communication Theory. (2014, July 10). *Interpersonal communication*. https://www.communicationtheory.org/interpersonal-communication/

person during a conversation, but it could also be a person's subconscious interpretation of a word or phrase.

Noise is the reason clarity is a major key to any conversation. The more clear you are the easier it will be for the other person to understand the message you are trying to convey. With a world full of all kinds of noise and disruption, the clearer you are the less the noise will impact your message.

Aim for the Prize

As a natural conflict avoider, I used to shy away from being direct. Whenever I was forced to face my fear, or stand up for myself, I avoided stating exactly what I wanted or exactly how I felt. While "That's fine" may be an acceptable response for choosing a restaurant with your friends on a Friday night, it is usually not the right response when a friend of yours asks if a certain behavior bothers you or if your boss is dumping loads of projects in your lap. You must be direct during difficult conversations to make sure the other person knows what you want or how you feel.

Do you remember going for a specific cereal box in the grocery store when you were a kid? Instead of choosing a cereal that you wanted to eat, you picked the cereal box that had a toy on the inside. Rather than eating the cereal slowly over a couple of weeks and hoping you would eventually find the toy at the bottom of the box, you went directly for the prize on the inside. That is what people want with tough conversations. They do not want you filling the conversation with fluff or making it seem like a lesser issue than reality.

I know you have something you want to ask for or something that is bothering you. You have something that needs to change. People want to hear your concerns directly without dancing around the subject. You can start a conversation with some general catch-up, but go straight for the prize in the box when discussing important issues. In Chapter 10, you determined a specific goal for your conversation. Be clear about your request or concern so the other person does not have to dig through your words to understand the real message.

Ask

Have you ever been frustrated that something is not coming to fruition? Maybe it is the fact that you didn't receive that gift you were dying for on your birthday or you haven't gotten a promotion at work. A lot of times we think that we deserve something or believe that we already asked for something from others. I had a conversation with my friend James recently where I told him about how an ongoing situation was not resolved in my life. He simply responded, "Have you asked for it?" At that moment, I knew that I hadn't asked for the very thing needed to change my situation.

While you may be sitting and complaining about the amount of work on your plate or that a friend has not invited you to *The Bachelorette* watch party, you may not have asked for what you want. If you want less work on your plate, then you have to ask for less work on your plate. If you want to get invited to your friend's watch party, then ask to be invited. The situation may be that your boss does not realize how much is on your plate or your friend accidentally forgot to invite you.

If you want something it cannot hurt to ask. One of my best friends, Christopher, has a strategy when he goes shopping or out to eat. Often when he goes to a restaurant or store he asks if they have any discounts. During our time together in college, which is a convenient time of life for student discounts, the cashier would sometimes create a discount just because he asked for one. If you want something, you have to be direct about it and you have to ask for it. People will not go out of their way to offer you a discount or invite that they are not aware of themselves. You have to make them aware of what is on your mind.

Avoid the Spray

I'm cursed. Every time I take a road trip I end up driving through a rainstorm. Dating back to my permit days, I am always the one to drive through the rain. When my brother, Austin, and I went on road trips in college, I always drove through torrential downpours while he had perfect sunshine and clear skies. He slept peacefully riding shotgun, while I white-knuckled the steering wheel through the dark hills and mountains of Tennessee during a monsoon.

As a self-proclaimed rain driving expert, it is better to stay away from cars around you during a storm. It is always nice to have taillights to follow ahead of you, but if you get too close to the car in front of you, the wheels spray up extra water and dirt on your windshield. People sit in the same lane behind other cars because they feel safer, but it is actually quicker and easier to see if you move to an open lane. Once you hit the open lane, there is less anxiety and less worry because you have clearer vision moving forward.

A difficult conversation is like driving on a wet highway. The more you spray someone with nonsense and fluff, the harder it is for that person to understand what you are trying to say. They do not have a clear picture of your goal or message. Say it, don't spray it. Speak directly and clearly to make it easier for the other person to understand.

You can avoid extra fluff in a conversation by avoiding "… but …" The "but" limits the praise inserted earlier in the statement.[30]

For example:

"I really like the way you wrote this section of the report, but this part needs to be redone."

"Your hair looks great, but your shirt doesn't work with that outfit."

In these sentences, conjunctions like "but", "however," and "although" limit the praise at the beginning of the statement.

---

[30] Sterling, K. (2018, October 25). *Eliminate "but" from your vocabulary when giving feedback.* Inc.Com. https://www.inc.com/ken-sterling/eliminate-but-from-your-vocabulary-when-giving-feedback.html#:%7E:text=When%20giving%20feedback%2C%20avoid%20conjunctions,'and'%20in%20your%20phrase.

Instead of thinking about the high quality of a section in the report or how great their hair looks, the other person is distracted by the constructive feedback in the rest of the statement. Some people believe "but" completely removes any comments mentioned before the word, but I believe it limits the positive enforcement. Those conjunctions don't entirely take away the praise, but they do distract the person from any positive, legitimate encouragement you provide.

Alternatively, try using the following phrases:

"I think this section of the report is awesome. I have a few recommendations about the introduction to help make it perfect."

"Your hair looks great, and I think a blue shirt would match better with those shoes."

Subtle tweaks can take a possible strenuous conversation to one with positive, accepted feedback.

Simplify

As mentioned earlier, I was given a project at work where I needed to prepare company information for a meeting with an internal partner. It is really easy to go to a company website, pull the description, and call it a day. Unfortunately, website descriptions can be so complicated that someone at their own company may not be able to tell you how the firm makes money.

When I turned in my first draft of the project, the banker brought it over to my desk to tweak some things. As we walked through some of the line items, he asked me a question about a company description, "Do you know what this means?" The description was so confusing from the website that I did not understand how the company operated.

For illustrative purposes, I will use an example about a bicycle shop. The website may say, "retail monetization of dual cylinder self-propelled vehicles." In reality, the shop sells bicycles.

The banker gave me a great piece of advice: describe the company as if you are explaining it to a child. Now when I put company descriptions together, I know that I need to make it very clear how the company operates and makes money. The same principle applies when I have difficult conversations. I have to be clear about what I want to change or the other person will not understand.

In your conversations, describe your desires in simple terms. You do not need to talk over someone's head to appear superior or knowledgeable. Explain your concerns, feelings, or questions in a way that others can understand. It makes it easier for others to help you. Donald Miller, a marketing and business expert, says it best in his tweet, "Cute and clever don't make money. Clarity makes money."[31] Instead

---

31   Miller, D. [@donaldmiller]. (2017, October 11). *Cute and clever don't make money. Clarity makes money.* [Tweet]. Twitter. https://twitter.com/donaldmiller/status/918141146899079168?lang=en

of creating cute or clever words to say in a difficult conversation, keep it simple.

Dating

My best friend Chase and I led a devotional group in college with some of our teammates. One semester we spent each week talking about dating and relationships because college guys care about relationships but commonly lack the vulnerability to hold real conversations. We walked through the book *Single Dating Engaged Married* by Ben Stuart. The book highlights numerous tips to help young adults throughout the dating journey, one of which is the need for clarity in a relationship.

While Ben was pursuing his now-wife, he was very clear after every date about his intentions and feelings. His wife was never in the dark about where he stood. In contrast, some of the men in our devotional group did not know how to be clear with their intentions or did not care enough to share their true feelings with the women they were taking on dates or spending time with on campus. In today's dating culture, men and women are rarely straight-forward or honest about their feelings or intentions. Many teenagers and young adults fear labels and set up a hang-out with someone they find attractive without indicating whether it is a date or not. Eventually, young adults end up getting coffee or studying with each other for weeks but one person does not realize the desire of the other to pursue a relationship.

Your conversations should not be like a college student's dating life. Be clear about how you feel and where you stand. If you want a get-together to be a date, then call it a date. You will save weeks of energy and effort if you are honest at the beginning.

In the workplace, if you are happy with your boss and job, then say that. If you feel overwhelmed physically and emotionally because of your work, then be honest. Honesty, even though it is hard, is the ultimate clarity in a conversation. Assess the situation and determine if you should be honest.

Communication is key for any relationship. Any job, relationship, or team is going to have bumps in the road. The more clear you are during the storm, the easier it will be to set the course straight.

Leave with Understanding

Early in my professional career, I used to sit in my boss's office and take notes as he or she gave guidance on a project. Instead of leaving the office with a total understanding of the task, I would listen and act like I understood everything completely. I would leave the office just to realize that I never understood the instructions. Does that sound familiar? Instead of speaking up and saying that I didn't understand how to complete the project, I acted as if my boss had communicated everything effectively. My behavior resulted in more questions and back and forth for the team. I would go back to my boss multiple times just to get the same question answered or have him or her explain the same problem in a different way.

Instead of me saying, "I don't understand this, can you explain it again?" I would remain quiet and say everything is fine. When you have a conversation with instructions or tasks to be accomplished, make sure that you leave understanding everything that was said. Do not leave the conversation with more questions than you started.

Tip: If there is part of a conversation or instructions that confuse me, I repeat the words back to the other person as if I am giving instructions to them. For example, I say, "Let me make sure I understand. I need to calculate the following numbers and send them to Tiffany. Is this what you meant?" The repetition and question show the other person whether he or she explained the instructions correctly and indicates if I understand what needs to be done.

Repeating instructions back to the other person increases clarity between the two different parties. It eliminates back and forth and noise that happens from one point to another. Clarity is key to any difficult conversation

Key Phrases:

- "I don't understand this. Can you explain _____ again?"
- "Let me make sure I understand correctly …"

Remember:

- Clarity is key to properly transfer a message from one person to another.
- Be clear about how you feel and where you stand.
- Avoid conjunctions like "but," "however," or "although."
- Repeat instructions back to the other person to avoid future interruptions.

Questions to Ask Yourself:

- Have I been direct in my communication?
- Does the other person clearly understand what I am trying to say?
- Have I specifically asked for what is needed to change my situation?
- Is it best to be completely honest in this situation?

Scenario:

You are a woman and there is a man who is interested in taking you on a second date. You went on one date and are not interested in another because you don't feel compatible. When the man is talking to you about the second date, you come up with excuses and say you are busy. You don't respond to his texts for hours on end and assume you give clear hints that you are not interested, but he keeps trying to schedule a second date. What do you do next? (Hint: I don't recommend ghosting.)

CHAPTER 12

Take Ownership

During the large team meeting referenced earlier in the book, the athletes' goal was to get a bunch of things off our chests and share frustrations to get the team on the same page with the coaches moving forward. Frustrations ranged from the training plan to travel meets and everything in between.

I knew that I wanted to talk about the communication between the coaches and the athletic training staff. Running is a sport full of injuries, and many of my teammates, including myself, needed lifting modifications to avoid injury and protect our bodies. It would have been easy for me to sit down, look the coaches in the eyes, and command, "You need to do a better job of communicating with our athletic trainers to get the best weights program for the injured athletes." Instead of placing all of the blame on the coaches, I took part of the ownership. Many of us took ownership in our approaches by asking what we could do better, and it set up a better, more controlled conversation.

I asked, "I've noticed that we've had some communication issues between the coaches, the weights program, and athletic trainers. I feel like I'm left in the middle with unclear instructions on what needs to be done for my injury-prone body. I'm wondering what I need to do better and what we can do better to work together to make sure that we're all on the same page."

To my surprise, instead of getting a list of different things that we could be doing better, coach simply responded he can do a better job at communicating and that was it. I admitted that I wasn't doing everything 100% on my end and that showed appreciation for the other person and what he was doing. Someone doesn't want you to come up and just blame him or her for everything that's going on.

A relationship is a two-way street. One person is not pulling all of the weight, so a lot of times a big issue in someone else's hands actually falls on you as well. It is important to acknowledge your part and take ownership in any conversation that may be difficult.

Admit Your Mistakes

In *How to Win Friends and Influence People*, Dale Carnegie highlights a number of great tips to communicate with others. In Part 4, Be a Leader—How to Change People

Without Giving Offense nor Rousing Resentment, of his best-selling book, a key principle is to talk about your own mistakes before criticizing the other person.[32] By taking ownership of your mistakes, you show the other person you recognize where you have fallen short.

The Paycheck Protection Program has been an ongoing ordeal for banks since COVID-19 took over the world. The "PPP" is a forgivable loan program in multiple government stimulus packages that helps companies cover payroll expenses to avoid massive job loss in the U.S.

Companies all over the country were upset because funding disappeared in just a couple of days during the first round of funding. The government threw the project on banks in the U.S. and they were forced to develop systems and processes overnight to try and support government loan applications. Naturally, the process took a long time to get right and every bank had clients that were concerned or frustrated about the status of their loans.

I had a client leave me a voicemail where he sounded frustrated and annoyed because he had not heard anything about the status of his application for a couple of days. During the stressful time period, companies were worried about applications and wanted to be in the loop every day to know if they would receive funding. He let me know that he felt left in the dark and ignored.

---

[32] Carnegie, D. (1998). Talk about your own mistakes first. *How to win friends and influence people*. Pocket Books. pp. 203-207.

After debating whether to send his number to someone with more client-facing experience, I decided to return his call. After introducing myself, I immediately apologized for how he must have felt as a business owner. I acknowledged that this process would make him feel left out and said that I would want to know more about my application if I were in his position. I recognized that our company should have done a better job of keeping him in the loop and pointed out that we had employees working night shifts to keep up with everything going on.

When I recognized his concerns, he loosened up. He thanked me for admitting that and was not upset with me in any way. He said that it would be nice to know more, but he understood why it was taking so long when it was involved with the government. The conversation ended on a happy note, and we got to know each other a little bit after talking about his application.

Taking ownership of the problem sets other people at ease. Someone may come into a conversation "ready to fight," and when you take some part of the ownership, that person will naturally let down some of their defenses. Instead of pushing back, they realize that you are willing to work with them and make yourself flexible for the better of the relationship.

Dr. Marisa Franco, a psychologist and policy fellow at Millennium Challenge Corporation, credits this phenomenon to the Law of Reciprocity. "People respond to us how we respond to them."[33]

---

[33] Doares, L. (Host). (2020, February). Avoiding conflict is worse than facing it [Audio podcast episode]. In *Happily Ever*

When you take ownership of an issue or problem, the other person becomes more willing to admit fault and take ownership for how they acted. People feel a greater obligation to respond the way you respond. If a friend of yours trips and falls, there are two common responses: immediately help or laugh. If you are in a group and witness a crashing to the ground, you will react similarly to the group. If everyone laughs, you feel an obligation to laugh. Your words influence how others respond. Taking ownership invites vulnerability to push the conversation constructively forward instead of leaving you in a defensive battle.

My Favorite Question

There are thousands of opinions on how to effectively lead teams. You may read one book that has a simple three-step formula for the perfect team or another on how to best communicate with different people. At the end of the day, there is no perfect way. There is no magic formula to make your team more effective. Everyone's leadership style is different, and every person responds better to different tactics.

Over the last six years, I ran for both good and bad coaches. I worked for bosses who connected with me and others who kept their distance. Some show great leadership ability, while others lack what is needed to motivate a team or

---

After Is Just the Beginning. Spotify. https://open.spotify.com/episode/7l2YFCct1Bir3x6AuhMLLX?si=SSltwjdKTDG-OH-d5XTU7BA&nd=1

company to perform well. The best coaches and bosses I had each asked this question:

What can I do better for you?

That is my favorite question. During a college internship, my boss asked me that question after the first week of getting settled into my project for the summer. That one question set the tone for a great summer because I knew I could be open and honest with her about how we could work effectively together. It was not just hearsay, because she showed me the entire summer that she was willing to fight for me and her team.

This question shows two things:

1.   Humility. You admit that you are not perfect. There are many leaders who struggle to admit they do not know the perfect way to run a team. You must set your ego aside to ask what you can do better.
2.   You care about your team. You are willing to adjust how you are doing things to help your teammates perform better. You want to see them succeed and are willing to make necessary changes.

This question is not exclusively for leaders, managers, or coaches. Anyone can ask, "What can I do better for you?" Asking this question as a young professional shows a person you are willing to grow and adjust.

Asking for feedback is difficult. I don't ask how I can improve enough because my ego gets in the way. I like to think

I know how to do my job, so I don't ask because I want to avoid the reality that I could be doing something wrong. I know that isn't the right mindset if I want to continually develop.

If you have employees/teammates/athletes who are willing to ask what they can do better, you will see your team operate together at a high level. Employees feel appreciated and open communication flows when honest feedback is recognized and applied. This can help teams at work, friendships, and romantic relationships. It takes incredible humility to admit that you could be doing better and even more to follow through on the feedback you receive.

Make it Easier for the Other Person

A mentor of mine, Will, is a man full of great advice. I was fortunate enough to rotate with his team for seven weeks and we worked on multiple projects together. Will and I worked together on a project for a client that involved different teams at the bank. In the beginning, we struggled to get support and help from others while trying to serve the client. After a call that did not get us anywhere, Will looked at me and told me that we have to serve the information up on a platter for others to approve. While it was not our area of expertise, we did a ton of research and contacted internal and external partners to get what we needed to ultimately help the client.

We had to take ownership of the issue because other teams didn't have the time to help. You must take ownership of your behavior and performance. If you are constantly seeing the same issues over and over again in various jobs, then there is one consistent piece—you. While you may have a tough boss or rough company culture, you have a lot of ownership over your day-to-day interactions.

Email is the most common form of communication for a number of employees. On a given day, I see hundreds of emails giving instructions or making demands. Some emails rub me the wrong way while others open a dialogue. When I send over a recap of a presentation I put together or analysis of account information, I leave it open to discussion instead of stating that my way is the truth and only path forward.

I hate it when someone tells me that his or her answer or instructions are the only way to do something, just to realize that person was incorrect. A couple of phrases I like to say in written or verbal communication to avoid that situation include: "Let me know if I missed something" or "This is how I interpreted the information." The comments show that I spent the time to put together assumptions or analysis, but admit that adjustments could be made. The words make it easier for the other person to build on what you created.

We all know people who think they are right 100% of the time who never admit fault. No one wants to work for or with someone like that. Take ownership of your mistakes and take responsibility for any changes that need to happen. Have the humility to accept corrections or additions. You may be causing part of the conflict in the relationship that you don't realize.

Key Phrases:

- "What can I do better?"
- "I'm sorry for the way you must have felt."
- "Let me know if I missed something."

Remember:

- Take ownership of your mistakes.
- A relationship is a two-way street.
- Make it easier on the other person.

Questions to Ask Yourself:

- Am I part of the problem?
- What can I do better in this situation?

Scenario:

You are a team captain. Your team is usually a top contender in the conference but has fallen short the first half of the season. The team is constantly arguing about nothing important and you are all frustrated at the team's record. You host an athlete-only meeting to let the team vent about team performance and struggles to get refocused in the right direction for the rest of the season. Knowing that you are part of the problem, how do you approach the athlete-only meeting?

CHAPTER 13

Create a Common Goal

ugust always brought me feelings of excitement before every school year. As a college athlete, I always got to return to the stomping grounds before the other students showed up on campus. Like many teams, the cross country team would spend a week in training camp before the school year and season started. Training camp is the time to bring the team together and get to know our new teammates while setting a vision for the year.

We spent a lot of time on campus, but we would always go and spend a couple of days at a retreat center outside of Nashville. Team activities included swimming in a large pond, kayaking, exploring rural Tennessee on long runs, and some of us even got bitten by a dog. Training camp was a time more than just running together; it became an environment for bonding as friends.

This uninterrupted time was crucial to center the team on the season. We spent meetings talking about our goals, looking at where we wanted to go, and also reflecting on where we had been. Every training camp resulted in the same non-negotiable goal: win conference.

Cross country may look like an individual sport to some people. You run by yourself and compare your race time to how fast you previously ran that distance. While there is an individual aspect of cross-country, there are even greater team goals that drive runners. At the end of the day, if you have a strong season individually, it fails in comparison to succeeding as a team.

In my junior year of high school, my cross country team qualified to the state meet for the first time since our school moved up to the largest division in Illinois. We lost a couple of our top runners going into my senior season, but we still had a strong team with expectations of returning to the state meet. We three-peated at Conference and had a number of strong showings and individual personal records throughout the year.

In Illinois, you must place in the top five teams at Sectionals to qualify for State. Senior year, my brother and I both placed in the top ten, and we stood at the finish watching as our teammates crossed the line. As each guy passed, we had no idea whether we would qualify as a team or not. In a heartbreak, our team ultimately fell five points short of qualifying for State. The hardest part about placing 6th overall was our 5th runner ended up falling in the middle of the race, which was the difference between us qualifying to the State meet. While it was nice to qualify for State as an individual with my brother, it hurt more to miss out on that goal as a team.

Goals

Team goals are often better motivators than individual goals because you prepare weeks, months, and years with other people to reach a single pinnacle.

Goals will vary for different teams. For a sports team, goals often look like winning a game, conference championship, or a national championship. For a sales company, goals often look like a certain sales or revenue goal. For a distribution or logistics company, goals may be a certain number of packages sent out of a facility per day. For a college, it is pretty easy to set goals for average GPAs, but new goals could relate to the number of courses offered or a certain news ranking in the country. Every team has different goals based on the nature of the business, but the presentation of the goals can vary as well.

For example, Clemson football chooses a theme or word for the season, beyond their national championship aspirations. Jon Gordon, Jimmy Page, and Dan Britton wrote *One Word*, a book about choosing a word to focus on for the year instead of, or in addition to, a New Year's resolution. This is not just for individuals, but teams now choose words to gather around for the year.

Your team's goal can help shape your approach to a difficult conversation with a teammate. Large team goals, words, or phrases act as drivers for behavior and action throughout the year. Use them to address something that needs to change.

For example, what if your roommate and his friends make it too loud for you to sleep almost every night of the week? When you lose sleep, you find yourself crankier and less effective at work. When you talk with your roommate, share how the noise has affected your sleep and work productivity, but it can help to add how that lack of sleep affects your relationship with your roommate. That may be your mood around him or a lower desire to clean common areas.

When addressing conflict, you need to speak the other person's language. If you blabber on about your side of the story, there becomes a point when you lose the other person. They may respect what you are going through and acknowledge what you are saying, but there is a missing piece in your demands or requests if you only talk about yourself—the other person.

Subconsciously, people think about how a specific change will affect them. If you talk with your boss about your lack of productivity, she is thinking about how her overall team numbers may be down for the quarter or year. You have to speak her language by addressing how your struggle affects her team results. Discuss how your lack of productivity and inefficiency may cause delays that force projects on your boss's plate. Discuss the fact that you are so exhausted from the work day that you show up to the office late and miss out on prime work hours.

Use the phrases below to indicate you are working towards the same goal:

"___ will help our team in the long run." Insert a specific change you are proposing.

"For us to _____, I/we will need _____." Insert a team goal and then a change that would help reach that goal.

Speak the language of the other person in the conversation.

Win-Win Scenario

What is success in your eyes? Success may be financial freedom or a certain position at work. For another person, success could look like growing a family or plenty of free time to exercise and be outdoors. Success is different in the eyes of the beholder. Ultimately, that version of success is the driving force for someone's actions throughout the day. If someone wants to be financially successful, that drives the late hours at the office or the pursuit of a large paycheck. If another coworker desires exercise, then that explains why they leave work right at five to hit the gym.

In work, sports, and school, every single person's idea of success differs. On a sports team, it may look like an individual stat line or all-conference recognition. At work, your boss may see success as certain numbers or financial benchmarks for your team. It's important to know what success looks like for the people around you. If you need to approach a difficult conversation, then you want to speak into the other party's version of success.

When I approached a difficult conversation with one of my coworkers last year, I needed to set up the conversation in a way that aligned with his version of success. For him, success means working a lot of hours and performing really well in his job to support himself and his family. For me, I am driven by purpose and a healthier balance for the hobbies I enjoy in my life. At the end of the day, money is nice to have, but it is not a driving force for me to perform well in my job.

During my rotation, I was drained from working insane hours and a deal flow of never-ending projects. I had to tailor my conversation to show that I could work more effectively if some changes were made to my schedule. In an effort to work a more regular schedule, I told him that in order to be the most effective and productive while at the office, I needed to leave earlier for the next week. The conversation went really well because I showed him the value my changes would add to his version of success. I explained how a little break to avoid burnout would help the quality of the team's projects in the long run.

Speak to the other person's version of success to create a win-win scenario.

I'm on Your Side

My friend, Robert, is an incredible photographer and creative. As a freelancer, he has jumped around with different companies and jobs over the last few years. Years ago, he created graphics and photography for a furniture company. As time passed in his contract, he realized that he was providing a lot more value and work than his compensation.

Contract negotiation is a common struggle for freelancers, including the difficulty of how much to charge for various projects. To receive fair compensation for his work, Robert talked to his boss about a raise.

At first, his boss did not take the conversations well and was shocked that he would be asking for more money because she perceived that he was paid enough. Robert has a phrase he uses to eliminate unnecessary tension in a conversation, "You realize I'm on your side, right?" He directed his golden words at his boss, and she immediately shut down her defenses and ultimately ended up agreeing to a raise three times his current earnings.

I love the phrase that he uses: "You realize I'm on your side, right?" That phrase shows that you are looking out for your best interest but also looking out for the other person's best interest as well. It shows your willingness to collaborate, but you also know your worth.

If the other person does not understand where you are coming from in a conversation, use the phrase, "You realize I'm on your side, right?" to soften the environment, lighten the mood, and open his or her eyes to the realization you are on the same page.

Key Phrases:

- "I'm on your side" or "I'm on your team."
- "____ will help our team in the long run."

Remember:

- Create a common goal.
- Team goals are greater than individual goals.

Questions to Ask Yourself:

- Where can I create common ground?
- What goal(s) do we have in common?
- What is the other person's version of success?

Scenario:

You are an NCAA Division I soccer player. Your team is top three in the conference with a legitimate shot of advancing to the NCAA tournament. Your body feels beat up from a long season of tough practices and you know that you need to take a step back to be fresh for the important games in the season. Who are you going to approach and what will you say?

Step 5
SPEAK UP
- - -

Take Action.

CHAPTER 14

Tips to Help You Speak Up

N ow you have the tools to approach and navigate a difficult conversation in your life. You know why it is important to speak up and why it is common to shy away. You have the tools to prepare your heart, consider the environment, and word your conversation correctly.

At the end of the day, the preparation skills will not do you much good if you shy away from the conversation. As someone who is a natural conflict avoider, I struggled to speak my mind and share how I felt. I struggled with the step to overcome my own fear.

Here are a few practices that will help you conquer your fear of conflict.

Accountability

When I started college, I let people walk all over me and eventually realized that I couldn't keep living the same way. My college roommate and best friend Chase is the best person I know about facing conflict head-on and standing up for himself. I always wanted a piece of his fearlessness and courage to face the conversations I shied away from for years, so I went to him for help. Whenever I had someone I needed to speak to that scared me, I let Chase know. Even now that we live in different parts of the country, I text or call him to tell him I have a big conversation coming up. He encourages me and also gives me the accountability I need to follow through.

All he has to say is, "Let me know how it goes." That is enough motivation for me to make it happen. But Chase also holds me accountable to face my fears with more demanding consequences at times.

A few years ago, my brother and I each had conversations we needed to face. In an effort to force us to follow through, Chase sat us down in my dorm room and created a challenge. As college athletes, any type of competition is the ultimate motivator. Chase knew that it would take a lot of effort for me to speak up, so he decided on one of the worst consequences imaginable: laxative pills.

If my brother or I finished our conversation, then the other had 24 hours to complete his. If one of us did not complete the conversation within 24 hours of the other, the loser would take three expired laxative pills. Talk about a nightmare! Chase aimed for five pills out of pure cruelty, but I negotiated him down to three in an effort to keep my brother and myself alive.

Needless to say, I had an incredible amount of motivation to speak up. My brother took care of his part of the bargain in the first three hours, so I was stuck with 24 hours to tackle my demons. I found myself sitting outside of the student center the next morning contemplating my choice of friends while also wondering how miserable my life would be if I failed to complete my end of the bargain. Luckily, the person I needed to approach sat a few tables down from me and I knew it was time to make my move. 30 minutes later, I eventually mustered up the courage to sit down at the other person's table and hold a conversation.

My brother and I each held conversations that didn't go as we hoped, but we were both satisfied with speaking up for ourselves. I don't think I will ever be happier to finish a conversation than that day, even though it ended in a disappointing result.

Talking to a boss, asking a professor a question, or asking someone on a date each takes courage. Chase served as an accountability partner to me and forced courage out of me through a significant punishment if I did not follow through with what I promised.

An accountability partner helps push you when you do not want to move. Your friend or mentor can find ways to motivate you that you would not try for yourself. I am fortunate the person whom I took mental notes from and watched for years happened to be my best friend and roommate. You may have to go out of your way to find a friend who will be direct with you and hold you to a high standard.

Find someone who will hold you accountable for standing up for yourself and create a system that helps you conquer the conversations you fear.

Five Second Rule

Mel Robbins wrote a bestselling book, *5 Second Rule*, where she highlights a simple tactic she discovered to help her act.[34] It is simply a countdown from 5 to 1. You can count out loud or in your head, but you simply count 5 … 4 … 3 … 2 … 1.

Most of us know what needs to be done but struggle to actually take that first jump. Counting down in your head distracts you from any feelings of anxiety and shifts your focus to action. Once you are in motion, you are more likely to complete your goal.

Before a difficult conversation or anything that scares you, your mind focuses on fear. You think about the negative aspects or outcomes of the task in front of you. Psychologically, when you use this five second rule, you distract your mind from those negative thoughts and the fear holding you

---

[34]   Robbins, M. (2017). *The 5 second rule: Transform your life, work, and confidence with everyday courage.* Savio Republic.

back. Instead, the countdown shifts your focus on moving forward.

Mel discovered this trick through an impromptu countdown to get out of bed in the morning. It can be used for something as simple as avoiding the snooze button or as big as a conversation that you need to have with a friend, parent, or boss. When you sit trying to will yourself to move, try the five second rule instead of playing "what-if" scenarios in your head. You will discover that you will take action towards difficult conversations and take on other fears in your life.

The more you face fear on a consistent basis, the easier it will be for you to overcome the bigger challenges. Every time you have a difficult conversation or speak up, it makes it easier to act the next time.

When you sit across the room from someone and don't know whether you should talk to them—count down from five. When you sit next to someone but cannot get yourself to bring up what you want to say—count down from five. When you sit on your phone but cannot get yourself to hit the call button—count down from five.

Trust Your Gut

You know how to handle difficult conversations better than you realize. You know how to gauge how someone is responding to a conversation. You know what you need to say and how to hold yourself in a room. The last thing you need is a little shove to act.

I feared speaking up because I was worried the conversation would end poorly. I worried that a relationship would fall apart if I truly shared my concerns. Learn from me—I was wrong. Most of the times where I build up the courage to act and speak result in needed and beneficial changes. Most of the difficult conversations so far in my life went well and resulted in a stronger bond on the other side, which is the opposite of what I expected.

Some conversations will flop and cause greater tension and issues. That happens to the best of us. You won't navigate every conversation perfectly, but you also cannot control how the other person responds. You can prepare your heart, set the environment, and word the conversation correctly, but the other person may take your words in a different direction. Do not beat yourself up if the other person reacts irrationally. Some conversations will take that wild turn, but most conversations will go better than you expect. You will walk away surprised at how well a conversation ended rather than fuming out of frustration. People are not out to make you upset, they want to work with you.

Trust your gut when you need to speak up. You know when you need to say something and you know the words to say. I used to avoid necessary conversations or waited so long that I eventually suppressed my frustrations. Once I gained the momentum to follow through on what my gut told me, I approached difficult conversations more consistently. You are a few difficult conversations away from the momentum you need to speak up. Bring in an accountability partner or use the five second rule to help you take the first step you need.

Remember:

- Find an accountability partner.
- Countdown: 5 ... 4 ... 3 ... 2 ... 1.
- You cannot control how the other person responds.

Questions to Ask Yourself:

- Who is someone who can hold me accountable?
- What is my gut telling me?

Scenario:

Your professor asks for feedback on how she teaches class on a regular basis. In an open conversation, she asks the room to share any ideas to make the rest of the semester a better learning environment. You know that you want more hands-on examples but are afraid to share your helpful ideas. What do you do to help you speak up?

CHAPTER 15

Jump

At the beginning of 2020, my friend Peter randomly said to me, "We should go skydiving this weekend." Peter and I have very similar bucket lists, but a conversation had never resulted in either of us saying we should skydive in a couple of days. Since it was his birthday coming up in a few days and my birthday happened only days before, I was all in before I realized what I had gotten myself into.

Before I knew it, we were driving an hour outside of Atlanta about to jump out of an airplane at 14,000 feet. As anyone can imagine, skydiving for the first time is a nerve-wracking experience. The thought of free-falling through the sky with nothing but a parachute to catch you is enough to make the average person worried.

As you prepare to get in the airplane, the instructors talk you through the process of jumping all the way to landing on the ground in victory. Even though I knew my instructor was experienced, my palms were a little sweaty, my knees were weak, and my arms were heavy.

Skydiving is an incredible experience, but the anticipatory fear and anxiety had me going to the bathroom every 30 minutes. Once the plane finally arrives, the instructors plop you on a bench in a dinky piece of flying metal and take you straight up for 10 minutes. The ride is nothing like a commercial jet with armrests and a cushioned seat. Instead, you are strapped to the chest of someone you met 15 minutes beforehand. Before I knew it, my feet hung over the edge of a moving airplane at 14,000 feet.

You know that falling feeling you get when you wake up in the middle of the night? I expected to feel that sensation the entire time I fell, but to my surprise, it only lasted the first two seconds. After that initial jolt, I felt like James Bond or Ethan Hunt plummeting to earth on a secret mission. Skydiving was one of the scariest risks I have ever taken, but it was also one of the greatest experiences of my life.

Approaching a difficult conversation feels a lot like skydiving. You experience an incredible amount of fear and anxiety leading up to the point where you verbally speak up, but once you are in the middle of a conversation, you realize that it is not as scary as anticipated. Once you get past the fear of the jump, you realize the journey is worth the courage. You finish and say, "I should have done that sooner!"

Once you are on the other side of the jump, you see the person and situation from a new perspective and realize that you had no reason to be so terrified in the first place. Your fear was more of a problem than the actual challenge in front of you.

For most of my life, I sat in the airplane and never jumped out. I forgot that I had all of the tools needed for the challenge. I knew how to take off, control the descent, and land, but I never jumped. You now have all of the tools and skills you need to speak up. You recognize the fear and know what it is costing you to remain silent. You know that others cannot read your mind and do not know exactly how you are feeling.

Before a tough conversation, you know the importance of preparing your heart. It is best to assume someone is trying their best. Every situation can be seen from a different angle. Every person handles conflict differently, so it is important to get advice from others who have gone before you.

You know the importance of the environment. It is best to praise publicly and construct in private. Your presence is like a flag at the beach; waive the green flag to make others comfortable. Every situation requires a different approach and attention to detail.

Your words hold great weight. Determine your goal and what you want to be accomplished. Be clear about your request and make it known. Take ownership of any misunderstandings or shortcomings and create a common goal, together.

When you need the extra push, find an accountability partner and countdown from five. At the end of the day, you cannot control how the other person reacts. You can follow the framework perfectly to set yourself up for success and still have a conversation go sideways. You cannot control every aspect of how the other person will interpret a message. You will have times where conflict goes well, but you will also have times where you leave a conversation feeling utterly disappointed and that's alright.

Just like how you shouldn't let five bad minutes ruin an entire day, do not let one bad conversation ruin your perception of speaking up.

You are ready to speak up, all you need to do is take the jump. Get a friend to hold you accountable and count yourself down. You are one conversation away from being understood and respected. One conversation from the change you need.

It's time to speak up.

ACKNOWLEDGMENTS

This book would not exist without the help of so many great people. Thank you to my family for encouraging me to pursue my dreams. Thank you to the friends and family who read my Monday Motivation posts the last 4 years. Without your encouragement and support, this book may not be a reality.

Thank you to my best friends who encouraged me to write a book on this topic. You gave me the confidence to pursue a life-long dream.

Thank you to the dreamers who take action. You know who you are. The late-night conversations and phone calls push me to keep pursuing the dreams on my heart.

Thank you to Self-Publishing School and my coach, Brett Hilker, for your guidance during the entire book-writing process. Thank you to my editor, Sky Nuttall, for turning this into a polished product.

I wouldn't be the person I am today without the impact of so many great mentors, coaches, professors, teachers, coworkers, bosses, teammates, and friends. Thank you for shaping me into the person you see in this book. Your advice and guidance live in these pages.

CONNECT WITH JARED ONLINE!

Website: www.jaredpeters.co
Email: speakupbook@gmail.com
Instagram, Facebook, Twitter: @thenormaljp

CAN YOU HELP?

Thank You for Reading My Book!

I really appreciate all of your feedback, and
I love hearing what you have to say.

I need your input to make the next version of
this book and my future books better.

Please leave me an honest review on Amazon
letting me know what you thought of the book.

Thanks so much!

Jared Peters

FREE SCENARIO GUIDE

Want to test your communication skills?

The **Scenario Guide** outlines Jared's **Speak Up Framework** and 13 scenarios to help you conquer the difficult conversations in your life.

You can download the FREE Speak Up Scenario Guide at

https://mailchi.mp/bd84f78cb93b/speak-up-scenario-guide
or at https://jaredpeters.co/free-guide/

Made in the USA
Monee, IL
23 October 2021